Kant, Hegel

ROBERT ULICH *has also written*

Fundamentals of Democratic Education

and

History of Educational Thought

CONDITIONS OF CIVILIZED LIVING

CONDITIONS
OF
CIVILIZED
LIVING

by

ROBERT ULICH

NEW YORK · E. P. DUTTON & CO., INC. · 1946

AMERICAN BOOK—STRATFORD PRESS, INC., NEW YORK

TO

ECKART

Sub Umbra Alarum Tuarum

CONTENTS

ACKNOWLEDGEMENTS

I wish to acknowledge my indebtedness to Dr. Hedwig Schleiffer for helping with the research work necessary in connection with this book.

Also I remember gratefully many conversations with Dr. Habib Kurani about the problems on nationalism and international contact.

And, I wish to thank Dr. Mary Ewen Palmer, without whom this book would not be what it is now.

My thanks are due to the publishers who granted me permission to use copyrighted material from their publications which are duly noted by specific footnotes.

INTRODUCTION

THIS BOOK represents a bold attempt to answer the question
as to the conditions under which civilization is possible. In
one way or the other this question has already been asked by
historians, sociologists, and anthropologists. But most of these
studies approach the problem either too historically, or too
analytically. And whereas the historical method tends to remain too narrative, the analytical methods tend to isolate a
few clearly discernible factors from the totality of human life
and to forget that it likes to mix hope and disappointment,
achievement and failure, light and darkness, grandeur and
vileness, rational and irrational forms of behavior.

But if any generation of mankind ought to understand the
complexity of human nature and the vicissitudes in the history of human societies, it is ours. Who can help but be both
depressed and bewildered when he sees before his own eyes,
as it were, whole nations destroying their own tradition,
bestiality breaking violently through the layer of seemingly
sacred custom, and despair driving men toward insanity in
a world of potential plenty?

When man is confronted with such chaos as we have now
before our eyes, he can no longer be satisfied with partial
questions and answers. Rather we need to ask the most fundamental question we can raise with respect to the perpetua-
tion of human societies; namely, why and how it comes about
that whole civilizations and nations rise and fall. Then we
discover some fundamental social laws which, when obeyed,
make man productive; when disobeyed take cruel revenge.

These laws are closely linked to—or are perhaps the reflection of—certain permanent tendencies in human nature which are violently struggling for satisfaction. When blocked up, they flow into subterraneous channels from which, from time to time, they send their volcanic masses into the seemingly peaceful dwellings of men. In addition, it always happens under such unfortunate circumstances that the more subtle creations of the human mind, such as art, education, philosophical and religious thought, no longer provide a natural fulfillment of man's noble desires, but become unguided, imitative, or abstract and sophisticated, a "superstructure" rather than a part of the full stature and structure of humanity.

Naturally, if someone wishes to discover the essential factors in the growth of civilization he must not try to describe the multitude of details which constitute the social environment of man. Rather he must reach into this realm of human existence and experience which is both central, in that it affects the feelings and behavior of the whole personality, and common, in that all men share in it and need for it some form of expression.

Thus this book represents a study in fundamental human experience, or one could also say, a study of human existence in its most universal qualities.

In the first chapter I have attempted to bring forth a group of general physical and mental needs and desires which must be satisfied if man wishes to lead a productive and tolerably happy life. One may also say that this chapter deals with the most general and basic conditions of a healthy society.

A society is always more than the mere sum-total of its members. Nevertheless, it consists of individuals and depends, with respect to its own welfare, on their emotional balance and creativeness. Therefore an analysis of the conditions of civilization needs an attempt at understanding the processes which allow for the healthy growth of individuals. Consequently the second chapter of this book is devoted to a study of personality. Under which psychological conditions can a human being mature to the fullest degree of his capacities and develop purposes and loyalties which are of value not only to himself, but to his fellow men?

In this endeavor a person depends not only on the degree to which the basic conditions of civilization as described in the first chapter are materialized in his environment, but also on the historical character of his society. Which forces of the past have given mold and substance to the present? Are they in harmony with each other so as to allow a person to breathe in a sound cultural climate, or are they irreconciled and thus liable to create feelings of disharmony and bitterness? Specifically, are the social and spiritual conditions of our Christian Western civilization such as to give us hope for further development? In other words, must we consider the terrific crisis in which we find ourselves the foreboding of our end, or is it the purgatory through which we have to go in order to make our souls ready for new thinking and acting?

The belief in the latter possibility is identical with confidence in our capacity to harness for the service of humanity four great cultural activities more successfully than has been done so far: namely, education, the arts, politics, and philosophical and religious thought.

Consequently the last four chapters of this book are devoted to these activities.

No country, so far, has been able to reconcile the two goals of modern education, that is, to supply on the one hand some degree of cultural unity within the nation and, on the other hand, the full development of individual talent. Nor has any country solved the dilemma which stems from the twofold obligation of education; namely, to serve specific interests such as preparation for a vocation and for loyal citizenship within an individual nation, and to represent at the same time the universal values of humanity as a whole. Much of our present futile discussion about the contrasts between practical and liberal education stems from lack of insight into these deeper issues in education.

But the deepest reason for our present feeling of dissatisfaction with public education lies in the present lack of a generally recognized hierarchy of values which tells us what to put first and what to put last, and what, if deeply understood, can go together; and as, at least in such complex fields as education, there can be no good structural planning without a clear philosophy behind it, we have not yet built up a type of school which could show to the nation that there can be unity in a variety of educational goals, learning in connection with real experience, and responsibility and harmony between practical and liberal education. So far we have nothing but bad compromises. Therefore the chapter on education contains, in addition to more general considerations, a plan of a "School of the Future."

But it is a sign of narrowness or arrogance if educators presume that the salvation of the world is in their hands.

Education, like all the other conditions of a sound society, is not autonomous, but depends upon the health and productivity of the total civilization. Of course, there are the great educational geniuses, such as Comenius and Pestalozzi, who have enriched the fund of our cultural heritage as only a few great men have done. And there is many a modest little teacher who, unrecognized by the great world, yet constantly rewarded by the gratefulness of his pupils, is an artist and a benefactor of mankind in his own right. But the typical and even good teaching in our elementary and secondary schools, and probably in most of our colleges, is much more a process of conveyance and selection than one of original creation. The teacher, as it were, drops the pails down into the wells of culture, but the ever fresh supply is replenished by sources other than him.

Thus, if education wishes to live on itself, it leads toward desiccation and the overestimation of methods and technicalities, just as, to speak more generally, a whole civilization is bound to run dry if it relies too one-sidedly on only one of its resources, particularly on knowledge and information.

Here becomes evident the significance of art in our civilization to which the fifth chapter of this book is devoted. It is an offense if art is understood only as a decorative and pleasure-providing activity, or as a means of escaping the crude reality of life. Nor is art merely a way of emotional expression. Rather through the mysteries of form and symbol great art gives men the experience of nearness to the eternal truth and rhythm of life and, through that, a feeling of elevation and enrichment which despite all differences in style and approach places art in the neighborhood of philosophy and religion.

But though the best of what education and art have given to mankind stems from the life and imagination of individuals many of whom were unknown and lonely, both education and art need the communal interest and the group response of society to unfold their blessings fully.

A society thus responsive to education and art is one in which there is a high degree of political activity among its members. Politics is not only an affair of legislators and executives, rather it represents the sphere of civilization where ideas are constantly projected on the level of reality and application. This is especially true in our times of increased concentration of power in the hands of governments.

Hence the sixth chapter of this book is devoted to an analysis of the principles which must govern the thought and action of statesmen in order to make out of them guardians of civilization.

Much of our present political thinking and acting suffers from confusion with regard to two fundamental problems of organized society; the first has to do with the relation between the individual and the collective, the other with the relation between political ethics and political power. Unless we have clear concepts about these two all-permeating social issues we cannot develop a political philosophy to help us in the solution of the more specific tasks which are ahead of us.

What are these tasks? First, we must find a way to incorporate the modern sentiment of nationality and the right of minorities into social and international planning; second, we must use the growing political and cultural self-assertion of the masses for the broadening and deepening of national and international civilization, rather than living in a continual state of fear; and third, we must find a positive relation to labor.

It has been the central defect of our sociological thinking that, misled by false forms of humanism, we have considered these modern movements, especially those coming from the working classes, to be perilous to the great cultural achievements of the Renaissance with its emphasis on individual freedom. Instead we ought to have realized that the insistence of ethnic minorities and of so-far neglected social groups on a full expression of their energies is but an expansion of Renaissance individualism and the natural rights of man into ever enlarging social spheres, however perverted the forms of this insistence and expansion may sometimes appear. At present we are in a state of history when we must recognize, as the natural outgrowth of Western humanist civilization, the desire of all modern men of whatever social class for a full and decent life, and face this great obligation courageously; otherwise we had better prepare ourselves frankly and cynically for oppressive, instead of democratic, forms of society.

When we conceive of these great tasks of political thinking and acting we cannot but be ashamed of the haphazard conditions in which politics has remained so far. For rather than having a rational theory and practice of politics, we still live in a state of political alchemy. The great issue of the future, namely whether bolshevism or democracy will have the priority in reorganizing the world, is not so much one of merely economic or administrative structuring, but of greater courage in adopting a truly rational attitude, which is neither timid and romantic, nor merely materialistic.

No statesman can master substantially all the problems within the compass of his duty. He will have to ask for the advice of the men and women who have worked successfully in all the different fields which are described in this book as essential in the continual molding and remolding of civilization. But what can all the world's parliaments and all national and international committees do if nobody has at least a general vision of the essentials and the totality of civilized life, and if there is no unity of thought and convictions to propel all the various experiences and hopes of man toward a common direction?

Here, according to traditional belief, lies the particular function of philosophy and religion.

But this is the great question. To what degree can philosophy and religion fulfill this function? Philosophy has always done it for only a few, the Platonic or Aristotelian type of men who possess the strength and training of mind to sense the grace of the unity between human reason and the laws of the universe. Nevertheless, indirectly the many also profit, or are done harm, by philosophic speculation because it arouses their curiosity. In spite of all suspicion against abstract thinkers they are longing for the comprehensive mind who lifts their instincts, gropings, and aspirations up to the level of rationality. If he is faithful and courageous, they may accept this attitude from him; if he is destructive also then they believe him, perhaps even more because it gives them a flattering feeling of critical superiority over the simple man.

We live now in a period when men are again longing for comprehensiveness and catholicity of thought. But such qualities cannot be achieved without some metaphysics, or without some theology—if one dares use the term unhampered by its traditional connection with ecclesiasticism. For the principles which are necessary for a synthetic aspect of the problems of life cannot be found in strict and immediate experience. That is—to mention only one instance—the reason why the category of scientific exactness, so much admired during the last century, has failed to satisfy the gropings of the human mind. It has failed not because it is negligible—on the contrary—but because it is incomplete and insufficient.

However, what we need now is not a battle against science, as it is waged by certain neoromantic groups, but a new concept of philosophy or comprehensive scholarship which—as a revival of old though unfulfilled aspirations—would take into its stream of thought all that modern science, observation, and speculation can contribute to the understanding of man and the universe. The new philosophy must be catholic also in that it trespass both the regional and the dogmatic boundaries in which the traditional philosophic systems and institutionalized religions of the West have so far been imprisoned.

This universality, however, will not be achieved by a vague and abstract form of internationalism or by cutting off the characteristics of the organically grown forms of philosophical or religious interpretation of the world. To the extent that these characteristics are but narrowness and superstition their disappearance is certainly highly desirable. But in so far as they are symbols rooted in a particular mental climate, as certain trees and flowers belong to a particular landscape, their abolition would mean the fading of the color and concreteness which allow abstract ideas to express themselves in attractive language. It is the inner paradox of all great cultural movements that they can reach into heaven only if they have their roots in the soil. Taken out of it they falter and weaken like the giant Antaeus who could be defeated only when his feet no longer touched the ground.

Nor would a process of accumulation of all that a supreme philosophical or religious world council might consider worthy of preservation lead to a new philosophy or theology. We cannot change the great cathedrals of thought either into streamlined office buildings or into gigantic museums with an entire floor preserved for each of the great prophets and his followers.

Rather we must expect that the great systems of speculation—though invariably there are sudden survivals when people live in fear of catastrophes—gradually lose their impact on the minds of men, unless we are capable of building under and into their individual structures a common consciousness of the eternal verities which in spite of all individuality of expression will help men in all regions and civilizations to meet and understand each other.

But to what kind of fundamental content or common denominator can this universal philosophical consciousness be related? It is the reverential experience of the origin of all the separated forms of life in a deeper ground of existence. This experience embodies individual things and events into a great and meaningful order which takes away from them the curse of isolation and contains, in this way, an element of salvation.

The "humanist" tradition, characteristic of our Western civilization since the times of the Renaissance, is entirely dependent upon such an embracing metaphysical principle. For without it humanism runs the danger of separating man from the divine universe in and on which he lives. In which case the bitter line of the Austrian poet Grillparzer becomes true which says: "From religion to humanism, and from humanism to barbarism."

Tragically enough, the Christian churches, in contrast to the Chinese and Indian religions, have taught their followers that they alone can open the door toward this salvation. Thus these churches have not only failed to recognize the very element in Christ's teaching about the relation of all men to the "Father" and to recognize the fundamental world community of all great religions and philosophical systems; they have also split Christianity itself into hostile camps with all kinds of inquisitions fighting against each other.

It is not even necessary to separate large groups of so-called "materialists" and "naturalists" from the great metaphysical community of men, for their concepts of *matter* or *nature* contain also the idea of, and reverence for, a deeper principle of order within the flux of appearances. Instead of pushing their systems of thought into the limbo of the "atheists," from which they themselves answer with invectives against their inquisitors, one would do better to reveal to them their inherent idealism.

If one lays value on distinction and exclusion he has to exclude from the community of religious the mechanist who denies all freedom, the cynic who delights in the willful destruction of value, and the professional pessimist who sucks faith and hope out of human enterprise. Also another type of man has to be excluded from the community of the faithful, namely the sort of "idealist" who for the preservation of his personal peace and harmony flees into an artificial realm of ideas without any practical commitment to his less-favored fellow men. This kind of idealist together with the humanist without metaphysics, has built up the kind of intellectual or esthetic pseudo-aristocracy which has done as much harm to a truly liberal society as their professed despisers. For both neglect the quality of responsibility as an inherent element in constructive thought.

For providing substance and clarity with respect to the commitments and responsibilities which are ours, this book has been written.

CHAPTER I

BASIC CONDITIONS OF HEALTHY LIVING

IF, AMIDST this shattered world, we wish to preserve the goods of civilization for our children we must realize—even more, constantly materialize—the basic conditions under which a healthy and productive society can grow and persist. There must first be sufficient opportunities for physical survival, such as food, shelter, and warmth; second, there must be an opportunity to work; third, a people must have standards of excellence; fourth, a people must have the possibility to think freely and courageously; fifth, it must have faith; and sixth, it must have the experience of sharing and love. From these conditions depend all the other properties of a civilized life.

I. OPPORTUNITIES FOR PHYSICAL SURVIVAL

However much we consider man to be endowed with the gifts of freedom and reason, he is dependent upon physical circumstances with all their joys and limitations. Generally we do not think of these limitations as long as we are healthy and happy. Rather we delight in our appetite, in the strength of our muscles, in love and exuberance; briefly, in all that we may call the natural gifts of life.

But nature which sends into us the primordial gladness of being, forces upon us also the innumerable sufferings of all physical existence. All organisms carry in themselves the germs of death as an inevitable fatality. Death is the kin of life. Growth and rot, birth and death, joy and pain, are so closely intertwined that some of the great religions have placed death and suffering rather than life and happiness into the center of their thinking about human history.

But every organism contains the seeds of destruction not only within itself; it also causes destruction to other organisms. The profoundest tragedy of existence, more tragic than death itself, is that life must feed on life. Otherwise hunger cannot be satisfied. Being constantly driven by this, every animal, even every plant, has to devour something or will be devoured. And man, the "crown of creation," is not exempt from this law. Either he kills something, a plant, an animal, or even a neighbor; or he dies from starvation. From the biological as well as from the moral point of view, man is the most threatening beast of prey, for through the medium of intelligence he has developed preying into a highly systematic enterprise, and in contrast to animals, he applies it even to his own species.

Yet, though hunger, if not satisfied, is a menace as great and even more cruel than death, we have a different attitude toward each. Death is absolute and unavoidable destiny; no human can ever fight it with equal chances; we will never remove it, however much science progresses. There may be a stimulus even in death; for it forces man to think about perishability and eternity. But in spite of all speculation and religion, generation after generation of children will bury their parents, or parents their children. Hunger is different. Though it compels every individual to create demolition around it, hunger—we feel—is, together with all its negative sides, an integral element in the continual building up of life. Under sound social conditions, we enjoy it if our children come from their play or work and want a big sandwich, for then we feel that they are healthy. Those who can fight successfully their own hunger, can turn its rapaciousness into a stimulus and an energy. Therefore humans work, tame animals, plow their fields, and build factories. Today we hear from our economists that we are far enough advanced in agriculture and industry to save every man on earth from starvation, provided we really will it; in addition, all could have sufficient shelter and clothes.

It has been a long way upward toward this stage from the time when men still lived in caves, fought with animals for their daily food, and ate each other when there was nothing else available. But though we have today the knowledge and the tools to combat hunger, how is it in reality?

Some time ago I visited the exhibit of a convention where I saw a photograph of a line of hungry people waiting for bread before the doors of a relief agency. The text underneath the picture read: "Most of Humanity Know Only Hunger." My neighbor shook his head and declared that this was a lie. Certainly the text was false in a way, for even the hungry know something more than only hunger, unless they are in agony. But the statement is true if we interpret it in the sense that in the history of humanity more people have been exposed to starvation than have been free from it. One could just as well use hunger as the central scheme of a history of mankind, as concentrate on the role of wars, of great men, or of economic factors. Crop failure, exploitation and hoarding, lack of food distribution and transportation, and lack of relief organizations have always co-operated to work disaster on mankind, even in times when war was not the cause of a general disorder. Somewhere on earth people die from starvation every day, and every country on earth has periods of famine on its record.

It is not my wish to inflict detailed statistics, but even words which are heavy with content tend to escape our memory unless they are somewhat substantiated. So I have chosen to describe as compactly as possible some of the major phases in the continual failure of humanity to protect itself against the onslaught of physical catastrophes. Considering only the years since the beginning of our Christian era one could count several hundred great famines which from time to time have eradicated considerable parts of the population of one or the other country. To mention only some of the gravest: in the first decades of the eleventh century all Europe was ravaged by disastrous famines; in 1125 Germany lost perhaps one-half of its population from hunger; and as late as the nineteenth century, in the year 1846 to 1847, a famine in Ireland, due to the failure of the potato crop, caused 225,000 excess deaths to say nothing of a mass emigration to the United States. Russia has often been exposed to starvation, and in the years 1870 to 1872 Persia lost by hunger one and a half million people, a quarter of her population.

To India goes the dubious fame of being the classical land of famines, where whole provinces have been depopulated in every century. The toll of eighteen Indian famines between 1876 and 1900 was twenty-five million lives,[1] and according to Joseph Russel Smith [2] within "this century human bones have been taken to the Indian fertilizer factories by the trainload, because whole populations have perished, and not even the most distant kin of the dead remained on earth to bury them." At the end of 1943 the Indian provinces of Bengal and Travancore were again faced with an enormous shortage of food. Approximately 100,000 persons died of starvation in Bengal each week in the fall of 1943.[3] Expert writers state that somewhere always some thousands of Indians perish from lack of food even though it is not reported by official sources and even when the general crop conditions are satisfactory.[4] Many of the epidemics characteristic of India, as fever, dysentery and skin diseases, gain hold because of the physical exhaustion and previous emaciation of their victims.

But the so-called "advanced" Western nations need not look toward Asia. Before the second World War rich European countries proved unable to guarantee sufficient food to their children. Concerning the health situation of British

---

[1] William Digby, *Prosperous British India* (London: T. F. Unwin, 1901), p. 131.
[2] Joseph Russel Smith, *The World's Food Resources* (London: Williams and Norgate, 1919), p. 519.
[3] *New York Times*, October 28, 1943.
[4] John S. Hoyland, *Indian Crisis; The Background* (London: George Allen and Unwin Ltd., 1943), p. 170.

youth the Dean of Canterbury Hewlett Johnson [5] writes: "It is a sorry fact that millions of British children, on the day the war broke out, were seriously underfed, one-sixth of them disastrously so, as we were informed in a scientific study by Sir John Boyd Orr, our leading expert on food and health." But the situation of poor English children before the second World War was in most cases enviable in comparison to the malnutrition caused by the second World War on the European continent. Hundreds of thousands of European families are starving in consequence of occupations and blockades; and the enduring effect of undernourishment of children may be felt for several decades hence. In 1943 the report of the International Labor Office on the *Health of Children in Occupied Europe* [6] vividly described the starvation in Europe, which is threatened with depopulation and with the rise of a physically and mentally sick generation. With the peace we see that the situation is worse than even the greatest pessimist could have expected.

Even the United States, "the richest country in the world," had and still has many thousands of undernourished people. [7] In spite of all national wealth one-third of the population of the United States was, in the years around 1940, below the safety line with respect to the amount and quality of food. The result was general physical weakness, height and weight abnormalities, and diseases of specific organs. In evaluating these American data, one must, of course, not forget that part of the existing malnutrition comes from ignorance rather than from lack of food; in addition, the standards of American physicians with respect to nutrition are extremely high. Yet, from the point of the hygienist who wishes an optimum rate of health and efficiency, they are justified.

* * *

[5] Hewlett Johnson, *Soviet Strength. Its Source and Challenge* (London: F. Muller Ltd., 1942), p. 54.

[6] Montreal, 1943.

[7] Charles Biester in *School and Society*, 55:128-130; Margaret S. Chaney. "What Nutrition Can Contribute," in *Journal of Health and Physical Education*, 13:286-87, 312-314, May 1942.

What men in the course of history have learned to wrench away from hunger they have sacrificed to the Moloch of war. The more civilized mankind has become during the past two centuries, the more it has proved its incapacity of deriving lasting blessing from its own progress. While one part of humanity struggles toward the light, the other marches in or toward darkness and does its best to drag along the rest.

For a brief account of the terrors of war let us take only the period which begins with the French Revolution and which we call the "Democratic Era." The European losses caused by the wars of the French Revolution and of the first French Empire (1792–1815) have been estimated very differently so that it is impossible to give exact data. But it is safe to assume that they amounted to more than five and a half million losses of life in the armies and the civilian population of Europe.

One of the extremely bloody wars in comparison to the total number of soldiers was the American Civil War from 1861 to 1865. According to one historian [8]—also here the estimates differ in many respects—the Northern army numbered 13,000 men at the beginning of 1861 and one million at the end of 1865. Of these were killed or died of wounds, diseases or other accidents 359,496 men. The army of the South was considerably smaller, but of it were killed, died of wounds and disease, and were missing 576,626 men.

With the exception of the American Civil War, the wars between the end of the Napoleonic period and the beginning of the first World War have cost the belligerent countries of Europe and the United States relatively few lives, about three and a half million, though there was no year without soldiers of these countries participating in war somewhere. Enormous sacrifices began again with the mechanical mass war of 1914 to 1918 which cost all together 11,115,000 lives in consequence of wounds and diseases.

[8] Samuel Dumas and K. O. Vedel-Petersen, *Losses of Life Caused by War*. Edited by Harald Westergaard (Oxford: 1923), passim. See also P. A. Sorokin, *Man and Society in Calamity* (New York: E. P. Dutton and Co., 1942), passim.

Computing the deaths caused by wars from the French Revolution up to the end of the World War I in 1918, one arrives at the formidable number of 20,115,000 lives.

The number of war losses would increase considerably if we had sufficiently accurate evidence as to the losses caused not only by wounds and diseases, but also by excesses of deaths and deficits in births caused by wars. We have an approximate estimate, in this respect, only in connection with the first World War. According to Warren S. Thompson [9] the losses of the 1914-1918 war amount to more than twenty-five millions, if not only direct casualties but indirect losses in the civilian population and potential losses in births are accounted for.

This loss of more than twenty millions indicates only a part of the suffering caused by the wars of the last four generations. In order to arrive at a realistic picture, we have to add all the grief of the relatives and friends of the soldiers killed, the destruction of wealth and welfare, of works of art, and of hopes greater than can be expressed by any material standard, the nervous shocks and the dislocation of men, and the inevitable spread of delinquency, prostitution, and venereal diseases. Who, furthermore, can measure what it means that in every prolonged war civilization loses the potential contributions of many of the best who could not only enrich the culture and prosperity of their own nations, but build lasting friendships among different peoples? Astonishingly enough, most historians who rightly deplore the lack of creativeness in the decades after the first World War do not take into account the fact that of the generation which around 1930 would have provided the leaders of England, France, and Germany, millions of the best had not returned from the battlefields. Therefore there were, and are, in these countries so many overaged men in leading positions, remote from the feelings and sufferings of youth, thinking in terms

[9] Warren S. Thompson, *Population Problems* (New York and London: McGraw-Hill Book Co., 1942), pp. 44-45.

of the nineteenth century and unable to understand and master the tasks of the future.

Taking into account all the damage and bereavement, one can imagine the tragedy which has come over the world with the second World War. The losses of life alone defy statistics, even in our statistical age; they amounted for the first three years, from 1939 to 1942, to probably twenty million and from that up to the end of the war again about twenty million lives.

If one adds to these numbers the millions of victims of starvation, sickness, bombing, atrocities, and enforced migration, one may imagine how many generations will have to work before the physical, mental, and moral damage of the second World War will be repaired, as far as it is within human power to do so. One fact is certain; if Europe, and the white race in general, allow once more such gigantic destruction of man and material, they will reach a state like that of the end of Antiquity. Then a completely new era in the history of humanity will begin in which no longer the Western nations, but Asia will lead. Future historians then, will state that the white race which had learned to an unheard of degree to master nature eradicated itself because of its incapability of mastering its emotions.

*   *   *

Future historians will also point at the astonishing fact that this same race had developed traffic within a hundred years more effectively than the thousands of generations before; yet nevertheless had been unable and unwilling to attack constructively the problem of inequality of population densities in the different parts of the world.

"More living space," to be sure, has become the pretext for recent kinds of imperialism on the part of the so-called "have-nots," as the denial of the danger inherent in over-population has been one of the many sins of omission on the part of the "haves." But apart from all these signs of imperialism—and admitting that density of population provides in itself no criterion of welfare unless seen in conjunction with climate, resources, industrial capacity and human initiative—even then one cannot deny the enormousness of contrasts in the spread of men over this earth. A mere *laissez-faire* attitude in this respect must spell new unrest and disaster for the future.

Canada, for example, is economically and culturally hampered because the number of its inhabitants is inadequate to its size, its resources and its means of transportation.[10] If we exclude the Northwest of Canada, the northern parts of the prairie provinces and of Quebec as too unfertile, there still remains a habitable area of 1,354,000 square miles. This accounts for a population density of 7.7 per habitable square mile.[11]

Of the 2,970,000 square miles of Australia there remains a habitable area of 1,725,000 square miles, the population density on each such habitable square mile being 3.8. Similar conditions prevail in large parts of the moderate zones of South America, not to speak of the climatically less-favored zones.

In an article by Richard F. Behrendt we find the following statements: "Latin America, with few exceptions (among them Costa Rica and parts of Colombia and Brazil), has no farmer class. This seems to me the principal reason why, generally speaking, there has not been and could not be popular government in Latin America thus far . . . In Chile even today two-tenths of 1 per cent of the landowners (not of the population!) own 62 per cent of the land. These seem fantastic figures, but they are true." [12] The result of such underpopulation is enormous wealth on the part of a few families with monopolistic agricultural and industrial enterprises,

[10] William Henry Chamberlin, *Canada Today and Tomorrow* (Boston: Little, Brown & Co., 1942), p. 318, et passim.

[11] A. M. Carr-Saunders, *World Population: Past Growth and Present Trends* (Oxford: Clarendon Press, 1936), p. 173.

[12] Richard F. Behrendt, *Land for the People*. Address delivered at the Conference on Latin America. Sponsored by the University of New Mexico, Albuquerque. 1943.

and poverty combined with cultural backwardness in the majority of the rural population. If a person has to travel miles to meet his neighbor, and sometimes scores of miles to a place with schools and other requisites of civilized life, he becomes inevitably superstitious, asocial and reluctant to any change and innovation.

It must be said in honor of Australia, that in consequence of the influence of labor organizations one danger of underpopulation, namely child labor, has been largely prevented and better educational facilities created. Yet, there remains the fact that Australia as well as Canada—even more than South America—has been hostile to immigration and liable to racial prejudices, with the effect that today Australia, with all its potential wealth and manpower, must be defended by other nations against the Japanese danger.

Japanese aggressiveness, just as German or Italian aggressiveness, is certainly the result of a strong imperialistic and militaristic attitude in the leading parts of the population which cannot be reduced to merely economic and physical factors. But it also stems, at least in part, from a danger arising from the very opposite of underpopulation—overpopulation.[13] Japan proper, for example, whose total area is smaller than that of California, has—against a 3.8 population density per square mile in Australia—a population density of 439 persons per square mile. But as the northern island of Hokkaido is relatively barren and consequently has only eighty-three inhabitants per square mile, a higher density exists on the remaining parts of Japan proper. It reaches 1024 per square mile in the province of Kajawa, though this province was, at least in 1936, without industry. But even in the highly populated parts of Japan there are many mountains which forbid cultivation.

If we pass over to India, we find that many Indian peasants and their families have to live from the cultivation of a piece of land not much bigger than a rug of ordinary size.[14]

[13] A. M. Carr-Saunders, *op. cit.*, p. 265.
[14] John S. Hoyland, *op. cit.*, p. 38.

If a high degree of overpopulation combines with unemployment and lack of possibilities of emigration, then people develop political restlessness, disillusion in the so-called blessings of civilization, hatred and a rampant desire for conquest. Thus, while one part of the world becomes inert and backward as a result of underpopulation, the other part suffers from the unreleased pressure of overpopulation. Sooner or later the explosion comes and throws all countries together into a state of disorder which could be avoided if the human race in its totality were possessed of more foresight, courage in planning, and mutual sympathy.

Even the most prosperous countries begin now to be troubled with the population question, particularly in their big cities. These cities with their unnatural life conditions are no longer capable of reproducing their own population. In 1920 the ratio of white children in the United States per thousand women in the age between twenty and forty-four was 341 in cities over 100,000 as against 477 in small towns and 721 in rural districts. In addition big cities breed criminality and, as a consequence of their merely mechanical culture, cripple the emotional life of their inhabitants as much and more, only in other ways, as the extreme loneliness and boredom of isolated country life.

There has never been a period in the history of the human race when it possessed so much power over nature, and so little power over itself. We are like a man who has amassed gigantic wealth, but overworked his health and brain in the process. In order to recover and enjoy his fortune he must first of all change his character and his strategy of living. But nothing seems to be more difficult for a human being than this. Reasoning alone does not suffice. Only under the effect of an overwhelming stroke, which may just as well cause still greater sickness, do men and nations alter their habitual course. Will the catastrophe to which mankind is exposed at the present help us all to realize the close connection between man's physical and moral existence? Or will, like after the last war, the majority of us again prefer a sickening complex of timidity and hatred to liberating action, and look for scapegoats instead of looking at ourselves?

II. Opportunity for Work

In order to wrest the daily food from his fields and the other resources of nature, man has to work. This was both simple and clear in earlier periods; for up to our modern industrial era there were generally not enough people to do the necessary labor. Consequently, those who were able to work but refused to do so were despised as parasites. With growing industrialization the curse of unemployment has befallen exactly the most industrious peoples of the world. To mention only some of the most important countries: at the end of 1931 the United States had 9,365,000 unemployed, i.e. 7.5 per cent of the total population; Germany 5,668,000, i.e. 8.8 per cent; Great Britain and North Ireland 2,958,000, i.e. 6.4 per cent; Italy 1,637,000, i.e. 3.9 per cent; France had only 1,381,000, i.e. 3.3 per cent; and Japan only 729,000, i.e. 1.1 per cent. If one figures that the people affected by unemployment are at least two if not three times as many as the unemployed persons themselves, then the percentage of the population suffering from unemployment was in the United States 15 to 22.5 per cent, in Germany 17.6 to 26.4 per cent, in Great Britain and North Ireland 12.8 to 19.2 per cent, and in Italy 7.8 to 11.9 per cent.

But being unemployed means not only being incapable of feeding oneself and one's family or becoming dependent on relief; it has consequences far beyond those of merely physical nature. For work is not only a means of procuring a livelihood; without it a healthy person degenerates mentally and morally. It provides the necessary exercise for his mind and muscles and saves him from the torture of uselessness, aloneness, and boredom; it also gives him the opportunity for integrating his various and often diverging urges and desires through provision of a permanent task and purpose. Thus his life receives regularity and order, and he himself receives a feeling of dignity.

Work connects man with his neighbors, it incorporates him into objective and super-personal fellowships without forcing him to surrender his Self. Rather the individual Self is realized in that way. For only through spontaneous activity can he attach himself to abiding values; without work being possible all converse about human ethics and sympathy is just idle talk and a frivolity.

If Christ says in the Prayer of the Lord: "Give us this day our daily bread," he could have said just as well: "Give us this day our daily work." Thomas Jefferson, while writing the Bill of Rights, lived in a predominantly agricultural society with sufficient work for every able-bodied person and a fair distribution of the different age groups within the total population which allowed the vigorous to support both the old and the young people in their families. Had he lived in our unbalanced world, he would certainly have added the right to work to the rights of worship, speech, press, petition, and trial by jury. For the rights of the Constitution are of limited value to a man who is denied the right of co-operating productively with his society. If an unemployed person is asked whether he would give up the freedom of worship, speech, and press for a decent job, he might choose the latter, though he would discover later that he can derive no real satisfaction from his work if it is not being done in a relatively free society.

The lesson we can learn from this dilemma is that no just society must expose a man to the crucial choice between work and the birthright of freedom; a society which does so is neither democratic nor free, even though it may pretend to be so.

And Esau said to Jacob, Feed me, I pray thee, with that same red pottage; for I am faint . . .
And Jacob said, Sell me this day thy birthright.

And Esau said, Behold, I am at the point to die: and what profit shall this birthright do to me?

And Jacob said, Swear to me this day; and he sware unto him: and he sold his birthright unto Jacob.

Then Jacob gave Esau bread and pottage of lentiles; and he did eat and drink, and rose up, and went his way: Thus Esau despised his birthright.

In this story from Genesis is revealed the cause of the surrender of nations to dictators.

In view of the degenerating effect of unemployment on the physical and moral structure of man, it is all the more deplorable that in the recent waves of depression the curse of unemployment has fallen with particular cruelty upon youth. In 1936 there were in the United States 4,700,000 young people between sixteen and twenty-four unemployed.[15] This means that over a third of this age group was running around, seeking desperately for some kind of useful activity or gradually habituating themselves to the material and mental effect of sloth. If this is not deformation of society, what is it? The fact that since about 1938 most countries have come out of the depression, is no reason to forget about it. For this country, like most of the other highly industrial nations, has escaped the final consequences of unemployment not through a genuine solution of the problem, but through the dire necessity of responding to the challenge of war with its enormous increase in production. Also in Germany the much admired miracle of reduced unemployment after 1933 was but the smoke screen behind which Hitler, heavy industry, and militarism prepared their onslaught on the neighboring countries and finally the misery of the same Germans whom they lured into their traps. But it is the declaration of total bankruptcy of a society if it finds itself between the despair of unemployment and the demons of war. Whatever has caused the calamity of the social pattern in which the upper and middle classes of the nineteenth century believed

[15] Maxwell S. Stewart, *Youth in the World Today* (Public Affairs Pamphlets, no. 22, 1938), p. 3.

because they profited from it, since the second decade of the twentieth century its failure has become evident. Also here we arrive at a conclusion similar to that in our section on physical survival; namely, that only courageous analysis of the causes of our afflictions and a gigantic practical effort toward reconstruction can save Western civilization.

But this effort would be doomed to miscarry if it ended in a form of social organization in which all other human concerns were swallowed up by economic interests. Man does live on bread and work at least, but he does not live on them alone. However indispensable sound physical conditions and opportunities for work are for the building up of a civilization, they alone cannot create it, particularly not for nations which have gone through the long struggle of man for the full development of his personality. Consequently we must reject both capitalistic imperialism and totalist collectivism, for both are inhumane. The first is in danger of solving the economic problem of man by making the masses dependent on the unrestricted reign of a few political and financial masters who rule the press and make public opinion, determine prices and wages and the chances for employment, use the state for their purposes, and—last but not least—make international politics according to their specific interests.

Nor can we submit to a kind of collectivism which engineers society as if man were nothing but an economic or political instrument. Certainly man cannot develop without feeling himself in the service of something which is greater than he. But at the same time he is an end in himself and endowed with rights which are essentially "inalienable," though their expression may be taken away from him by external powers. The true goal of economic organization can only be one which rewards man's labor through paying respect to his whole personality. It must enable him to live a life in which he eats his bread not like a slave, but as a worker among coworkers, however high or humble his or their status.

But a civilization which permits such an existence, can only be the result of continual accomplishment, watchfulness and maturity. It needs men who are not only jealous to safe-guard the more nature-bound conditions of man, but also proud of his spirit-bound qualities.

III. The Claim of Excellence

It is characteristic of all work which is done joyfully and with a certain hope for reward that it has in itself the demand for good quality. A worker who loses this incentive, be he scholar or artisan, does not remain on his level of achieve-ment but deteriorates. Just as well, a society as a whole needs the "claim of excellence" in order to persist physically and mentally.

There must be good craftsmanship, and it must appear on all levels of activity where human effort is able to improve the quality of work and things. We feel this sense for excel-lence in old furniture and folk art, in the gates of old houses —in the simplicity of their proportions, in medieval illumi-nated manuscripts, and in old penmanship. With a degree of justification, we may comfort ourselves for the loss of these preciosities by remembering that in our industrial age more people have a chance to enjoy some luxury than in older times. Many things have lost in individual quality, but they have become less expensive and therefore accessible to more.

It is even likely that today only the applications and lev-els of excellence in craftsmanship have shifted, and that in a romantic longing for perfection we glorify the past without enjoying what we have. Our forefathers, for example, did not know of the craftsmanship which a modern surgeon must achieve through combining a long scientific training with the highest degree of manual dexterity; they did not know the techniques used in a modern laboratory and in the planning and construction of a Diesel engine; nor did they know of the accuracy and thoroughness of research required from a modern philologist. But however useful and refined all these activities may be, the craftsmanship which is in them, is rarely surrounded by the aura of beauty and spirituality which accompanied the work of a Veit Stoss or a Donatello in earlier times.

But our trouble lies deeper than in the question of what some artistically endowed individuals do with their hands or their minds. It lies in the growing incapacity of our civilization to create standards of excellence which are of powerful reality in the life of nations.

In this respect, the United States of America is in a particular situation. This is true partly because this country has shown its greatest efficiency in an era of mechanical mass production which is not conducive to refined craftsmanship. It is true also because the founders of this republic lived in an understandable antagonism toward the European regime of absolutism, in which the concept of excellence was connected with an aristocracy as a special *élite* at the top of the society. With the development of the system of heredity it had become a sufficient certificate of belonging to the *aristoi* if one were born from parents with the title of nobility. Thus came about the curse of a privileged caste from which European society has suffered more than from any other social evil.

The American democracy, in righteous indignation against this European tradition, raised the banner of equality and of the natural rights of man—which also was a part of the European fund of ideals, but one which had remained in the spiritual sphere and had never become practical. In the democracy of Washington and Jefferson a fusion between the European monarchical and the American pattern was attempted; the *aristoi* of all social strata were invited to cooperate, though under the leadership of a gentry of somewhat hereditary character. With the Jacksonian revolution the bridge from the old to the new was destroyed. Men such as Emerson struggled in vain against the vulgarization of the great concepts of liberty and the natural rights of man into a kind of equalitarianism which looked with suspicion against the frank appreciation of merit, except when the clamor of a statesman, a victorious soldier or an athlete flattered the natural instinct for vicarious participation in fame and glory.

Curiously enough, the same equalitarians so often delight in setting themselves and their group off from "inferior" breeds of society of different racial or social origin. Some kind of hierarchy, some kind of keeping up with the Joneses and looking down upon the Johnsons seems to be a psychological necessity for many people.

However, beyond these antisocial desires for superiority, mostly connected with deep-seated feelings of inferiority, there must exist a possibility for social emulation, because most people learn the virtues of a good life not from hearing and talking about it, but from seeing and observing men and women who present to them the virtues of decency, of good manners, and of responsibility even to the degree of sacrificial leadership. It is dangerous to American democracy that the distinctions which have developed in its society, are often of no other than plutocratic character. Under such circumstances there develops the admiration for success and property as such and, with it, a perilous instability in social stratification, in contrast to the older European aristocracy, which was too stable.

The lack of a definite sense for standards shows most distinctly in the negligence of quality and thoroughness in our modern forms of education. Education is a very illustrative field for what we mean by a sense for excellence. It begins with extremely simple forms of habituating the young. The teacher who allows them to throw their coats into some corner—as if there were not parents who deprived themselves of many a pleasure to have their children clothed; the teacher who allows his pupils to do their assignments without diligence, in bad writing and in dirty notebooks; the teacher who himself feels at ease in a classroom which has no atmosphere of warmth and individuality; such a teacher, without knowing it, fails the younger generation. He misses the unique chance of forming habits which in later life may be the elements of great characters.

It is not progressive, but utterly deficient education, if under the principle of making learning more pleasant for children they are spared rigorous effort and thus deprived of the opportunity to sense the delight in real achievement. The great mission of progressive education lies not in acting on the lowest common denominator between ease and aspiration, but in applying better and better methods of motivation and of lessening the child's tension when he finds himself before a difficult task. Needless to say in connection with such endeavor progressive education has also to discover better criteria for judging the capacities of the child, for even the best methods are bound to fail which go beyond an individual pupil's compass of understanding. The aim can be only to achieve as much quality as is possible—but not less.

The scale of appreciation which the school develops ought to be twofold.

There is, on the one hand, the inevitable hierarchy of talent which, by some kind of divine dispensation, distinguishes men from men and which, according to Christ's parable of the rich man, ought to be cherished as one of the great obligations of humanity. However, those who have been given the talent ought to know that their distinction is not their merit, but the grace of nature for which they have to show their gratitude through ever increasing service.

On the other hand, there is also a hierarchy in the degree of effort by which every child shows his willingness to do his best. And this willingness ought to be rewarded as the achievement of real, voluntary distinction, thus giving even the less talented child a feeling of dignity and self-assurance.

We have mentioned the school situation—though it may appear to be somewhat petty in comparison to the society of adults—because it can serve as an illustration of the problem of excellence in modern democracy. Just as in the life of the school, so in the life of democracy there must be two levels of distinction. On the one move the men of unusual talent serving their country and humanity through applying their gifts in gratitude and responsibility for what they have received from nature; on the other move the men who, though modestly endowed, do their best at the places where they stand in our system of division of labor. Even though they are simple workmen, they nevertheless belong to the *aristoi*, or to the *élite* of their nation and should be esteemed much more than the man who has the riches of mind, property, and influence and does not use them adequately.

If our historical knowledge does not deceive us, some of the older caste societies so much despised by modern democrats had, at least before their degeneration, a finer sense for the various expressions of quality than our mechanized civilization. Perhaps we could even generalize and state that every good society has these two levels of aristocracy: an aristocracy of unusual talent in which heredity and good breeding may play their part, and an aristocracy of devotion which, however humble, enjoys prestige among all citizens for its social usefulness. Such were the conditions in the Athenian society of Socrates, in the medieval society of the free and proud cities, and in the American society of Benjamin Franklin.

In all these communities there was a sound mixture of balance and mobility; each citizen was conscious of the necessity of his individual contribution and, at the same time, participated in the functions and aspirations of the commonweal. With such a continual give and take the best features of democracy are existent, even though the governmental structure may be monarchical or hierarchical. Without it there is no democracy possible, even though the framework of the constitution may be avowedly democratic.

What greater offense can there be to democracy than that writers of radio scripts are urged by their agencies to abstain from ideas which are beyond the level of understanding of a twelve-year-old, or that Americans are constantly told that their average mental age is about that of early adolescence? All such statements do not realize that the mental state of an adult is not measured with respect to the criteria which may apply to school learning. Even if they did apply they ought to evoke the desire in all agencies responsible for the cultural level of this nation to lift the less educated on to the level of those who are better educated. No doubt this is the desire of every serious educator, therefore his alarm about the low standard of intelligence. But his endeavors are constantly frustrated by too many agencies—press, radio, and movie—which profit from dullness and vulgarity just as recklessly and joyfully as did the older feudal classes in Europe which were afraid to lose their influence with the increase of public schools. They all forget and forgot that a good society is a laboratory of progress and noble ambitions, not a playground for mediocrity.

But why is it so difficult in our time to preserve and improve older standards of excellence? Why, in spite of the increase of opportunities for education, are all countries looking desperately for leaders with broad and imaginative minds? How, in order to mention the worst of all possible examples of self-humiliation, could it happen that Germany, which for a hundred and more years had been prided on the best public school system, could fall under the tyranny of an Austrian adventurer whose style betrayed his confused and vulgar mind in every sentence, whose value system had been formed by a mixture of hatred, feelings of inferiority, and morbid ambitions, whose decisions were dependent on astrologers, and whose only distinction was the one-sidedness of an insane mind?

In order to answer this question we must refer to our previous discussion. For the continuous recreation of a sense for excellence, people need to live under conditions which give them at least a minimum of security and self-respect. In the night of despair every voice which spells promise is mistaken for the voice of a prophet, and every ray of light on the dark horizon for the first sign of sunrise. This is particularly true when people are no longer united by common ideals and consequently succumb easily to the neurotic temptations of a crisis. Faith in common ideals must have its roots in the ordinary life of the people, but it must also inspire the best in the nation; it must create loyalties which can be attached to persons rather than to abstractions, and which at the same time reach far beyond the mere tangible sphere of profit and interests. Because of this very necessity of a combination of the ideal and the concrete in the creation of social standards merely theoretical discussions do not help.

It is the most fundamental difference between thinkers and artists on the one hand, and great doers and religious prophets on the other, that the first group is venerated in a rather noncommittal intellectual or esthetic climate, whereas the hero and the religious prophet are emulated as examples of perfection. Children, as we know, do not improve morally because they learn about moral precepts, but because they identify themselves with parents, friends or teachers whom they admire. Adults are not different. In this sense we have to understand Emerson's statement in his essay "The Young American": "We cannot look on the freedom of this country, in connection with its youth, without a presentiment that here shall laws and institutions exist on the same scale of proportion to the majesty of nature."

Thus the sense for excellence, as any other important value, is closely connected with other factors in human nature which are also essential in the fabric of civilization. The two which are most intimately, even casually related to the urge toward quality, and to which we have already alluded in the previous discussion, are the faculties of critical judgment or reason, and of faith or hope. For only people who use their power of discrimination can develop a feeling for what is good and worth while or not. But they must use this power not only for criticism and analysis, but for constructive action which in turn requires an atmosphere of faith and hope.

IV. The Opportunity for Reason

In his classical oration on the character of the Athenians, from which we have borrowed the term "claim of excellence," the Athenian statesman Pericles speaks also of the power of reasoning as one of the conditions of an ideal society. He says:—

The great impediment to action is, in our opinion, not discussion, but the want of that knowledge which is gained by discussion preparatory to action. For we have a peculiar power of thinking before we act and of acting too, whereas other men are courageous from ignorance but hesitate upon reflection. And they are surely to be esteemed the bravest spirits who, having the clearest sense both of the pains and pleasures of life, do not on that account shrink from danger.[16]

One can generalize and say that all such historical periods were productive in which reason was respected as one of the highest qualities of man. This was the case during the centuries when Greece and Rome were flowering. It was the case in the thirteenth century when such men as Albert the Great and Thomas Aquinas used the weapons of the intellect, transmitted to them from Aristotle, for building up the intellectual edifice of medieval Catholicism. It proved true in the period of the Renaissance when the humanists prepared the minds for the analysis of both history and nature, and again in the eighteenth and nineteenth centuries when men, however defectively, applied reason to the problems of society and were so impressed by the power of the new movement that they believed themselves on the march toward permanent progress in spite of all the misery piling up in the substrata of their society.

In contrast, the decline of Antiquity is at the same time the decline of independent thinking. The end of medieval Catholicism came about when its leaders refused to include empiricism and individualism into their system of thought. The humanism of the Renaissance and the Reformation lost their influence on the European mind because they sold themselves too easily to absolutism both in politics and in the realm of the spirit. Finally, the rationalist liberalism of the eighteenth and nineteenth centuries suffered shipwreck when the modern bourgeois substituted capitalism for liberalism and preferred even the book-burning of the Nazis to facing the necessity of thorough economic and social reforms. When

[16] G. W. Botsford, *A Source Book of Ancient History* (New York: The Macmillan Co., 1912), pp. 207-208.

National Socialism unrolled the swastika banner over liberal Germany, its leaders included the fight against reason in their program.

It is no contradiction that the same leaders used technical intelligence more skillfully than it was ever used before, because isolated technical intelligence is not identical with reason. Rather it can be turned into a demonic power of destruction. Reason always aims at the totality of human relations; it is the integration of all the mental qualities in man which help him to realize the permanent in contrast to mere external advantage. Reason recognizes that every new progress toward reality or truth is only an approximation of the goal, but it sees its very dignity in the continual endeavor of the human mind to transcend its limitations. When this endeavor is abandoned, and man prefers indifference or cynicism to search, then he commits cultural suicide, whether he knows it or not.

The search for truth is not a phantom growing out of idle ambitions of the intellect, but the symbol of man's hope to intuit the laws of existence and thus to assure survival in the most comprehensive sense of the word. Societies which are not interested in understanding reality, and in planning and acting according to the conditions inherent in life, cannot develop. In all likelihood, they cannot even survive. And whereas reason always respects the variety of life, antirational societies prefer uniformity. For a while they may succeed in concentrating all their forces on one single purpose and thus, through their very one-sidedness, give the impression of an enormous vitality and efficiency. But sooner or later they get stuck in the bog of their own unrealism. Either they are overthrown from outside, or they create revolutions within their own boundaries, for they spread corruption and decay wherever they reign.

But no society is protected against the most dreadful fear which can befall man, namely the fear of reason. In his treatise *Of the Conduct of the Understanding*, John Locke distinguishes "three miscarriages that men are guilty of in reference to their reason." First there are people "who seldom reason at all"; second, those "who put passion in the place of reason . . ."

The third sort is of those who readily and sincerely follow reason; but, for want of having that which one may call large, sound, round-about sense, have not a full view of all that relates to the question, and may be of moment to decide it. We are all short-sighted, and very often see but one side of the matter; our views are not extended to all that has a connexion with it. This might instruct the proudest esteemer of his own parts, how useful it is to talk and consult with others, even such as come short of him in capacity, quickness, and penetration: for, since no one sees all, and we generally have different prospects of the same thing, according to our different, as I may say, positions to it; it is not incongruous to think, nor beneath any man to try, whether another may not have notions of things which have escaped him, and which his reason would make use of if they came into his mind . . . Here we may imagine a vast and almost infinite advantage that angels and separate spirits may have over us; who, in their several degrees of elevation above us, may be endowed with more comprehensive facul-ties: and some of them, perhaps, having perfect and exact views of all finite beings that come under their consideration, can, as it were, in the twinkling of an eye, collect together all their scattered and almost boundless relations. A mind so furnished, what reason has it to acqui-esce in the certainty of its conclusions!

Certainly, we humans are not such angels. Not only be-cause our mind is not "so furnished," but also because we are not even willing to use whatever "furniture" it has for pro-duction. Most of us live within a thick hedge of prejudices, the very characteristic of which is that they are not recog-nized as such but mistaken for substantiated and empirical judgments. Each period, it seems, cherishes its particular brand of opinions which have got stuck midway between complete irrationality and rationality. In earlier times they pertained to religion, but medieval man had apparently no racial prejudice. Now we have changed the role. In addition, there are many on whom the mere sound of certain political terms casts a spell preventing their brain cells and blood circulation from normal operation. We have not yet arrived at a stage of development when we dare apply scientific thinking to our political and economic problems, however much statistics we may use.

Thus, in relation to social life, many of us live still in a magic attitude, as older generations did with respect to nature. They were afraid of using lightning rods because they considered it an attempt at interfering with the will of the Lord; we are afraid of learning from the experiences of other nations because it may interfere with our own habits. But unless we get out of the age of unreason politically—as we may flatter ourselves to have done scientifically—we will never be able to direct the two streams of human existence, theory and practice, into one steady flow of reasonable action. We will continue to waste the lives of men in battles against enemies who could just as well be our friends, or in battles against a still more formidable foe, which is frustration of effort.

But, as we already indicated, reason needs the help of the best companion it can find, namely faith, in order to lead men into the fruitful fields of freedom and productivity.

V. Opportunity for Faith

Faith is the contrast to reason if we conceive of the latter as merely logical or technical intelligence and as a means of arriving toward exact statements about isolated phenomena. But if, with all due respect for accuracy and empiricism, we hold reason to be the power which renders man capable of transcending the immediate for the purpose of ever higher syntheses of comprehension, then reason and faith belong together. In historical reality, societies of reason have also been societies of faith, and societies of faith have also been societies of reason. The great founders of religions never conceived of a chasm between their prophetic teaching and the human search for truth. Even religious thinkers whose mission it was to interpret the revelation they had received from the prophets, such as Thomas Aquinas, strove for and held possible a reconciliation between faith and reason, though in the age of St. Thomas there already arose the problem of a "double verity," one divine, expressed in the Gospel and accessible only through faith; the other human, and resulting from philosophical reasoning.

The two verities became irreconcilable when the European institution which was regarded as the symbol of faith, namely the Church, could not reconcile its geocentric tradition with the heliocentric cosmology of Copernicus, with Newtonian physics, and with modern biology. Since then many modern men have become accustomed to the antithesis of faith and reason.

In the rationalist and idealist period for men such as Franklin and Jefferson, or Rousseau and Hegel, the word "reason" was still uttered with a feeling of reverence; there was, in spite of all hostility to dogmatism and denominationalism, still a religious aspiration contained in it. For these men had not yet forgotten the awe which arose in the scholars of the Galilean-Newtonian era when they suddenly discovered the miraculous connection between the human mind and the phenomena of nature they wished to understand. We no longer wonder at this invisible tie between the mind and its object; it is nevertheless not only the central condition, but also the central secret of all human thinking and experimenting. For if the astronomer, through a combination of observations and calculations can foretell what hundreds of years ahead may occur in the constellation of celestial bodies which the human eye cannot perceive, then there must be somewhere an unseen bridge between the human mind and the universe. Every great pioneer of thought builds a new bridge, with wider arches. But how would he dare do so if he believed that his mental planning were a merely individual venture? And does not an architect who plans a real and concrete arch across a river work with the same faith: namely, that his mathematical calculus, if performed correctly, conforms to the laws inherent in reality?

Only during our naturalist and positivist epoch the miracle has gone out of thinking, and reason has been understood as a mere tool in the search for scientific description. In consequence faith has become more or less irreconcilable with the demands of the intellect. It is difficult to say which party has suffered more in the conflict. In any case, our civilization has become like a seafarer who has lost his compass. For whenever the intellect wishes to unite isolated impressions in the vision of a totality, whenever man strives to integrate his instinctive urges into a productive purpose of life, he needs the directive impulse which comes from faith. However proud we may be of the wealth of data resulting from the devotion of generations of scholars to the most minute kind of research; however clearly we may discern the relation of cause and effect in the inorganic world and the reactions of the psycho-physical mechanism of animals and men; and however grateful we may be for the relief which through all these scientific efforts has been given to mankind; yet, if we wish to know what man really is, how to make decisions in hours of crisis and receive comfort in hours of suffering, faith in a comprehensive and meaningful universe is a greater help than all scientific analysis.

These convictions however, must not lead us into the lure of modern irrationalism and antirationalism. There are now, in an understandable reaction against the cocksureness of scientific positivism, schools of thought which use any scientifically inexplicable event as proof of the "supperrational character of life." But often there is nothing miraculous or "super"-rational in seemingly mystical events. Frequently men have despised reason only because they did not know how to use it. In addition, states of extreme excitement tend to engender such excessive activity of our vegetative nervous and glandular systems that they prevent the state of physiological balance in which thinking can take place. Nothing is more dangerous than to elevate any of these forms of failure or excitation up to the level of the superrational or religious. They may not be superrational but subrational. Confusions of

this kind have made it possible to surround all kinds of super-
stitions and mass hypnoses, such as excessive nationalism, political radicalism, and race prejudices with the halo of religion. But what people in that state of mind really are in, is
the most unsavory medley of ignorance, timidity, and aggressiveness; and no period of mankind yet has been completely free from it.

Often, however, irrational forms of behavior have lifted
men far above the normal human level. Through prayer and
ascetic practice the religious can work himself into a state of
trance and visionary ecstasy. If a modern man reads the
Fioretti of St. Francis of Assisi, he meets a group of saints
whose lives are completely outside the rhythm and impressions of normal men, without sleep, without sufficient food,
surrounded by angels and devils, haunted by pangs of conscience and fear of hell, or lifted out of earthly existence by
mystic converse with God, Christ, and Saint Mary.

The realization of the abnormality of such states of mind
has led modern writers to reject them as signs of insanity or
charlatanry. But normality and productivity are not the same.
If we admit that mankind needs the abnormal in order to
create the unusual, then abnormality, though negative from
the medical, may be positive from the cultural point of view.
The criterion is in the aspiration and purpose which motivate the extreme longing characteristic of abnormal persons.
Some rise beyond and above themselves and become examples of love, hope, and charity. Others fall below themselves
into the kind of terrestrial and demonic trance through which
a Hitler could set the world aflame.

But in both cases the human mind seems to be ready for
unusual decisions.

"Decision" is one of the most important categories for the
understanding of human life. We admire it in great personalities as the element without which all their other talents
would not have blossomed. As all terms of fundamental significance the word decision denotes widely varying experi-

ences. Every day we make a score or more of little decisions. We decide to go to our office earlier or later than usual, we decide to drink tea instead of coffee, we decide—for the fiftieth time—to stop smoking.

Here another characteristic enters into the picture. Decision, in order to be significant, needs to be lasting. Not without reason do we find in so many nations an adage which says that the way to hell is paved with good intentions. What are these "good intentions" but decisions without the quality of permanence? They are results of sudden feelings of fear, shame, failure, and thus, for a while, make a person open to new and extraordinary impressions. But when the shock effect is over the person closes himself to the unusual and the law of inertia sets in.

What makes it possible for a person to adhere to his purpose? There may be favorable environmental factors such as the approval of friends, reward, and prestige. But what if they fail to appear when the hour for greatness comes? Then only such a person can hold to his decision who is able to transcend the immediate and to believe that both he and his purpose are parts of a greater order within and for which they have to serve. This is faith. Our many little loyalties result from habituation, from interest, or from external pressure. But the decisions and loyalties which make history are not those which feed on external contingencies and profit motives, but those which live on faith.

In the *Wisdom of China and India* [17] a conversation between Confucius and Tsekung is reported. Tsekung asks Confucius about the conditions of government and Confucius answers: "People must have sufficient to eat; there must be a sufficient army; and there must be faith in the nation." "If you were forced to give up one of these three factors what would you go without?" asked Tsekung. Confucius said, "I would go without the army first." "And if you were forced without one of the two remaining factors; which would you

[17] *The Wisdom of China and India,* An Anthology Edited by Lin Yutang (New York: Random House, 1942), p. 839.

rather go without?" asked Tsekung again. "I would go without sufficient food. There have always been deaths in every generation, but a nation without faith cannot stand."

Confucius in this conversation speaks of a nation's faith in itself, not of faith in the more general sense in which we have tried to explain it. Yet—so he would say himself—how can a nation's faith in itself become something more than a narrow form of nationalism if it is not embedded in beliefs which reach beyond nations into ideas and ideals of still more comprehensive character?

Here is the point to confess that in our previous discussion of faith we have failed to discern different forms and levels of faith. We spoke of faith which is inherent even in the most scientific reasoning in so far as the scientist believes in the connection between his mental operations and an unseen reality of truth. We spoke of faith as a more or less sociological and pragmatical phenomenon, reaching from man to man or spanning the arch between the present and an expected future. Finally, we dealt with faith in a definitely religious sense. The question which thus arises, is this: To what degree must faith, in its quality as an essential condition of civilization, be nourished by transcendent or supernatural ideas, or, to what degree can it relate to merely human and natural ideals?

This question must be asked for several reasons. One may doubt to what degree our civilization, after a continual decrease of transcendentalism since the Renaissance, possesses sufficient religious dynamic to recreate constantly faith in things transcendent. Even if we think that our society is still religiously productive, does Christianity in its traditional form contain sufficient vigor to fill the transcendent desires of man with blood and energy; or, if not, what kind of faith should take its place? There is some reason for lack of confidence, not only because of the decrease of transcendentalism to which we have already alluded, but also because the Western nations have always been unoriginal, so far as religion is

concerned. They have either created some polytheistic folklore in which only historians can develop an intense interest,
or they have revived the prophetic heritage of Asia. To be
sure, the great philosophical tradition of Europe is not without transcendent dynamic, but it has been of more intellectual character and without the fascinating symbolism of the
Asiatic religions.

But if there is no religious rebirth possible, will the Western nations be condemned to live in the twilight of unfulfilled religious desires and technical intellectualism, until the
so-called Christian Western civilization perishes from earth,
or will they produce a full civilization with sufficient hope
and faith, without resorting at all to supernatural ideas?

The practical answer to this question will be most decisive
for the future of Europe and the world. Will Auguste
Comte and his followers be right who tell us that religion
and even philosophical metaphysics are but earlier phases of
human history, signs of the immaturity of man which do not
allow him to stand mentally, as it were, on his own feet? The
problem becomes all the more exciting as now, for the first
time within the boundaries of Christian civilization, a political society has arisen which intends to build its future on a
merely natural foundation, namely Soviet Russia with its
particular interpretation of Marxism.

Concerning Russia we are faced with a phenomenon of extreme psychological complexity and one too young to permit
definite judgment. Has Russia been capable of carrying
through her atheistic experiment because the people of Tol-
stoi and Dostoevski are so imbued with the religious spirit
that it works even within an atheistic philosophy and vocabulary? Then we would stand before the paradoxical situation
that Christianity shows its strength most insuperably exactly
among those who went out to destroy it. Or has history sent
the Orthodox Church from Czarist corruption into the cata-
combs in order to prepare the resurrection of Greek-Russian
Christianity in a transfigured state of purity and modernity?
Or are the signs of revival of the Christian religion in Rus-

sia which we now observe but the last flickering of a dying candle? And were the bravery and loyalty of the Russian soldiers results of a faith which is so strong just because it has no supernatural elements in it, but is based on concrete social experiences within the bolshevist pattern of life?

Whatever the answer may be, the majority of the Russians apparently believe in their mission to construct a new society with a degree of happiness and productivity such as was never created by peoples of the past. In spite of all professed atheism, this is a form of "secular transcendentalism." It remains on the social plane and refuses to go into the depths or heights of metaphysics. Yet, it too transcends the life of the isolated individual and of society in its immediacy both in time and space. Thus there is faith also in this kind of society, faith even of an immense intensity; but on its horizon there stands not the kingdom of God, but the kingdom of man.

Some may believe that this is the very kind of society which man of the future needs. Others will contend that a society which possesses no transcendent vision of man cannot even be a "humanist" society. Because of the lack of channels through which to relate itself to the Eternal, it will lose the challenge of permanent criteria of human life and get stuck in itself. And this has always been the beginning of barbarism.

Whatever the answer of history to the Russian problem may be, there will always remain true Goethe's statement that "throughout the history of the ages there runs one fundamental theme, so profound that it dominates all the affairs of man, this is the eternal conflict between religious faith and worldliness."

VI. Love

One of the reasons why our society has difficulty in maintaining in its social order a sound mixture of flux and stability, of mobility and contentment, and with it a wholesome hierarchy of standards, lies in the obstacles which it creates to sharing. Partly the modern division of labor is responsible for this situation; it has created specialization and mechanization. One could, however, contend that some forms of mechanized production have increased sharing through collectivization of work. Despite the fact that in a modern plant the worker is physically together with more people than the artisan was in the old workshop, he neither sees the finished product, nor does he, except in rare cases, feel himself personally related to the totality of the enterprise in which and for which he works. In spite of all the noise of men and machines around him, he is in an emotionally abstract situation. The same is the case with the wealth accumulated by modern industry and finance; it too is of rather abstract nature. In contrast to the property of earlier times, which consisted mainly of land, the new wealth is highly changeable, impersonal and flexible; it can be shifted from place to place; its bearers can create new fortunes through telegrams and after-dinner conversations, or lose millions overnight by the more skillful speculations of a competitor.

Lack of sharing is characteristic also of modern politics. Compare the modern delegation of power by the individual citizen to government officials and parliamentary representatives with the assemblies of the people as they were customary in some Swiss cantons up to some decades ago. We citizens of a big country vote for somebody whom most of us do not know; we believe in his ideas, or in his party, more than in another party. However, it is difficult for an honest representative to promise to his constituency adherence to a specific program, because the national or international scene may change the next year and require completely new decisions. Even within the local communities we rarely find real communality and sharing in management.

What is true of the economic and the political situation applies also to the activities of the mind. In certain fields, especially in the theoretical sciences, the creative scholar addresses only a small group of experts; even with his family and his friends he cannot share his work. Of our finest writers and poets only a few have a large public; though they show to man his own image with all its hopes and failures, the ordinary reader prefers to float in a stream of thrill and sentimentality which does not allow him to see the depth below or the sky above him. The church, which in earlier times claimed to give unity and dignity to the individual and his community, has lost in influence.

This statement concerning the lack of sharing at the present does not mean to say that the life of earlier times was necessarily more harmonious and sympathetic than ours. The old patriarchal landlord often exploited his tenants not less than the knights of early capitalism exploited their workers. Absolutist governments of the past gave their subjects certainly less share in molding their destiny than modern democracy, and popular education allows more people to enjoy the products of civilization than was the case in years gone by. Each period has its specific troubles. Ours is in the increase of atomization, and consequently in the decrease of sharing the joys and griefs of life which gave members of simpler societies a feeling of mutuality in experience and of hanging together in spite of all differences of class and estate. Our trouble is also in the loss of common symbols, rites, and beliefs which could relate people, in spite of all their differences, to a deeper and common source of inspiration. Merely social relations take the place of one common vertical relation of all men to the Absolute; we live beside each other, but no longer together.

Here lies one of the most crucial issues of American church life. Even in a small American community of a few thousand souls there is not one, but at least five churches. Their ministers are overwhelmed by activities in social clubs and welfare agencies. In their effort to avoid the verbalism and remoteness of older theology, partly also out of the necessity of competing with the rival churches, they now become absorbed in the innumerable trifles of social obligations. Others become interested in the actuality of politics to a degree that some modern sermons remind us more of the essays of a columnist than of worship.

Certainly, a one-sided tendency toward religious speculation, mysticism, and asceticism may establish a chasm between theology and the practical obligations of a Christian. It may separate the kingdom of God from the kingdom of earth so that the two can never come together, for if the Eternal is only "above" and not at the same time "within" our temporal life, it is nowhere. On the other hand, rash intervention of ministers in our present political issues may jeopardize the clergy's very possibility of representing the unchanging principles of Christianity amidst all the transient conflicts of man and thus prevent them from exercising the deepest kind of influence they could have otherwise. Then Christianity would lose in spirit more than it would gain in actuality. If, in addition, the common man discovers that the trends in ecclesiastical opinions about politics coincide strangely with the external interests of the churches themselves, or the governments of their countries, then the spiritual life of a nation becomes rife with suspicion. This was the historical situation out of which sprang the Protestant revolutions in the sixteenth, the French revolution against Catholicism in the eighteenth, and the breakdown of Russian orthodoxy and German Protestantism in the twentieth centuries. The political theologian can inspire men to believe in him only if amidst the struggles going on in the arena of politics he represents to them at the same time the Absolute in its eternal and uncompromising character, as was the case with Bernard of Clairvaux, Saint Francis, Luther, Calvin, or Ignatius of Loyola. They shared, and inspired people to share, in danger and sacrifice not because they mingled, but because they lifted up.

The importance of sharing is not sufficiently appreciated if we understand it primarily as an opportunity for each of us to cut his slice from the sweet cake of life. Joining in joy is easy and needs no discipline; that which creates community is the willingness to join in suffering.

This willingness, however, cannot be created artificially. No one can acquire a universal feeling of sympathy to mankind and nature, unless he has first experienced love in concrete personal relationships. There seems to be one basic requisite in the natural development of lasting attachment as well as in resistance against the bitterness which may accrue from the hardships of life. This is the love between mother and child. But it has as its physical condition another phase in the eternal cycle of Eros, or of loving relationships. This is the love between man and woman. The more it is rooted in deep sexual unity, the more mature and profound it can become; the more it can also become a reflection of the beauty of creativeness which expresses itself not only in the embrace and fertility of the bodies, but also in the embrace, friendship and unity of the souls. For love is both receiving and spending. And if the desire for spending becomes all-permeating it can create a feeling of cosmic sympathy which goes beyond all human boundaries and limitations.

The New Testament calls it *Agápe*. It is most beautifully expressed in St. Paul's letter to the Corinthians: "Though I speak with tongues of men and of angels, and have not love, I am become as sounding brass, or a tinkling cymbal." To some men cosmic love comes as an inexplicable gift of grace. Most people never achieve it. For them love is dependent upon, and bound to, specific persons and experiences. But the greatest prophets of mankind were those whose power of love was no longer attached to one or several single objects, but embraced all mankind, until they saw all things growing and living in an eternal hymn of universal creativeness. They took on their shoulders the burden of mankind and became the creators of new civilizations. Whenever men lose the mystery of cosmic love or the admiration for this mystery, then they also lose their faith and community and must wait in loneliness and despair for a new savior of mankind.

VII. Concluding Remarks

Two questions may be raised with respect to the foregoing attempt at defining the basic conditions of civilized life.

First one may ask which of the aforesaid conditions is the most important. The answer is: none; they are all of equal importance. Out of the fallacious separation of the elements of communal living have arisen all the futile arguments of philosophers and historians as to whether this or that supposed element of civilization is causal to all the others. With particular intensity they have argued whether *matter* or *mind* is more fundamental and, consequently, whether we ought to believe in a materialistic or an idealistic philosophy of history. Certainly, the problem of the relation between matter and mind opens up a metaphysical enigma of utmost importance which the human mind will never stop pursuing in spite of all the cautioning whispers of the methodically trained intellect.

But whatever the answer may be, in human development and culture the two things which we call mind and matter belong together. Separate one from the other and creative life ceases to exist. Reality itself, as we experience it, gives the pragmatic sanction to our assumption of an interaction between mind and matter. Surprising though it may be to many who believe in the speculative systems of naturalism, or materialism, or idealism, or all the other "isms"—for the understanding and progress of civilization it is much more important to accept humbly and admiringly the work of Nature and Spirit in us and in the history of the universe than to think that through the endeavors of our limited intellect we can break the doors to all the arcana of existence.

Secondly, critics might doubt the completeness of our list of the basic conditions of civilization. Completeness is a goal difficult to achieve; its aspect varies according to our standpoint both in space and time. Often the desire for external completeness but obscures the sense for the essential. Yet, one may rightly query why, for example, justice is not mentioned in our list, though Plato in his *Republic* considered justice the foundation of a sound state and society. We are, of course, far from denying the importance and dignity of justice. But at the same time we contend that justice will never grow nor persist without food, work, excellence, reason, faith, and love, whereas their existence will induce man to do justice as far as his natural weakness allows.

The same is true of such great historical concepts as liberty, or equality, or democracy. They all are results, even relatively late results in human history and have grown only in proportion to man's ability to create the basic conditions of civilization of which we have spoken. They could also be called the coronation of the human endeavor toward a dignified life. We may write and read thousands of books and articles, and deliver and hear edifying sermons about the sacredness of the human individual and of a "free and just society." Yet nobody will become convinced unless he feels that the men he is supposed to listen to are willing to pay the price for the blessings they recommend. This price is nothing but the willingness to provide for the nations of this earth—and not only for our people, but for all peoples—the conditions of a civilization as we tried to explain. The lack of courage after the first World War to provide these conditions made all the great announcements of a new democratic order and all attempts at a league of nations abortive. So also our present endeavors in political and educational reconstruction will end in disillusionment unless we build the new society, nationally and internationally, on pillars which have their foundation in the real nature of man and society.

CHAPTER II

CONDITIONS OF HEALTHY PERSONAL GROWTH

I. Challenges to Psychology

CIVILIZATION EXISTS only in and through the life and work of the millions of individuals who populate this earth. The well-being of each of these individuals is contingent upon the degree to which the basic conditions of civilization, as described in the previous chapter, are realized.

But however much the individual may depend upon the objective conditions of civilization there is a highly subjective factor in the use which a person makes of them. Each human being lives *in* the world and is a part of it; at the same time he is set off from it and has to plan his own role. And the more he is a person and has personality, the more he feels his separateness—sometimes as a blessing, and sometimes as a curse. When, according to the Hebrew legend, Eve and Adam ate the fruit of the tree of wisdom, "and the eyes of them both were opened, and they knew that they were naked," they lost that feeling of unity with the things and animals around them which we humans still have in the period of infancy and to which we sometimes dream ourselves back as into a paradisaic state.

Nothing should be easier for us than to explain the qualities of a human person, because each of us represents one. Yet, it seems to be the most inscrutable object for science and meditation. One of the reasons for this mystery of human individuality is that, in contrast to our being able to stand apart and observe from outside such things as minerals, plants, or chemical reactions, we can acquire only relative perspective to our own selves, because each of us is identical to his self.

In addition, the existence of the ego is only part of a greater miracle, namely of existence as such. Why do I exist exactly in the form in which I exist? Why does existence split into many diverse existences, ordered by man into such categories as *genera* and *species* with innumerable intermediate and special divisions? How does life flow into the different organisms? How do form and shape enter into, and combine with, growth? In other words, why and how does an acorn necessarily grow into an oak tree, and a human egg into a human being, male or female? What is the essence of these different human qualities, which we describe as instincts, urges, emotions, volitions, and reason? To what degree are they of innate and hereditary, to what degree of acquired character? Or, are they perhaps not at all different in essence, but one and the same fundamental energy showing different reactions to different stimuli? Perhaps the greatest enigma of individual existence is exactly the one which occurs in each of our mental acts: How are our so-called senses, our nervous system, our brain and glands related to our mind? We have, so far, no satisfactory theory concerning, say, the genesis of a word-concept or the interaction between the physical manipulations of a string quartet and our perception of profoundly meaningful music. It is not impossible that with further development of our insight into the laws of the universe we will suddenly have the clue. But before this happens we do not know what such elementary processes as "experience" or "learning" really are, though our life consists of them. We can only describe, but not explain, what we feel and think about our mental interior.

The fact that concerning all these questions we are still in a kind of pre-Galilean state explains the confusion which reigns not only in the problems, but even in the vocabulary of psychology. For how can we unite on a specific and unambiguous terminology if there is no clarity about the substance behind the words?

Thus the attempt, made in the following chapter, at explaining and understanding human personality, is hampered by an embarrassing number of uncertainties. There is nothing available but unreliable word symbols which represent shades, phases, and effects of the great phenomenon of Life as it realizes itself in the form of a human person. However, these word symbols are the only means we have for communication.

II. The Four-fold Human

If—remaining first within common experiences—we inquire into the character of our own and other personalities, we discover "at the bottom," as it were, a group of unreflective drives and urges which older psychologists used to call "instincts." We no longer like this term because it reminds us of a number of false conceptions which were in vogue in earlier times. The instincts were supposed to be "innate" and rather inductile. There were whole lists of such instincts, each instinct neatly separated from the other. And there was considerable argument whether they were inherently good and could, consequently, be relied upon as ingredients in the making of a desirable personality; or whether they were inherently bad and had to be "broken" before a human creature could become a decent man and a good Christian. The whole theological doctrine of hereditary sin is based on the, relatively realistic, opinion, that we never can rely on what these so-called instincts may do with us.

In order to avoid the old mysticism of instincts we now use other terms like "vital urges," "drives," "propensities," or such pompous terms as "unreflective behavior patterns"— still without knowing what we are really talking about. But whatever term we may use we could perhaps unite on the following definition which I now venture. There exist in all normal persons certain fundamental and vital "urges," which are closely related to the self-assertive tendency inherent in all life. If we pretended to diagram human personality, the "urges" would have to be put in the exact center of an expanding circle.

Some of these urges are innate, like hunger, thirst, and sex; others are acquired in the course of a normal life, such as the aggressive, gregarious, and protective urges. One could also say that these urges operate on different levels. Thirst and hunger are certainly nothing but expressions of the most primitive necessities of nature, and appear therefore right with the beginning of individual life. Others, such as the sexual, are of more complex nature and, therefore, appear relatively late, at least in conscious and mature form.

It may help to clarify the highly controversial character of the nature of these urges if we attribute to them three common and closely interconnected criteria.

First, they relate man most closely to animal life. Through them we all participate in the struggle for survival and happiness with all its vicissitudes. They remind us constantly that the "rational character" of man is built into a large arational foundation.

Secondly, these urges are common and develop in a relatively equal rate of progress and intensity in all persons whom we call normal.

Thirdly, we do not consider this development an accomplishment of special merit, but we expect these urges to appear naturally in the course of time. If they fail to do so we are troubled and suspect that "something is wrong." We have, for example, no special schools for the training of the "urges," as we have special schools for the training of the skills or the intellect. Only for abnormal persons do we establish special institutions which might be called schools for training in normal living.

But this "naturalness" of our instinctive life ought not to lead us into false feelings of security. Under certain circumstances, our urges may become "sublimated," but when offended or twisted they may betray the whole primordial brutality of suppressed nature. Or, like people in subjected nations, they may go underground and from their ambush take revenge for maltreatment through exercising a tyrannical and demonic power over the seemingly most remote areas of our physical and psychic life.

In their very nature, however, our urges are neither moral nor immoral; what they wish and need is a decent amount of satisfaction. The old theological and educational problem whether man is born good or evil is based on a fallacious premise. Rather we ought to think that his urges are multiple in character. A frustrated life renders a person's urges inharmonious, or obstinate, or even criminal. On the other hand, if the environment of a person fosters the exercise and satisfaction of his basic desires in individually and socially desirable forms, provides the right mixture of effort and reward, and allows him to breathe in an atmosphere of confidence, then he may turn the natural strength of his instinctive life into the most helpful instrument for the creation of a personality, capable of active sympathy for all that is great and constructive.

Hence, though we cannot have special schools for the training of our urges, because they ought to grow spontaneously, they are nevertheless constantly under some kind of training; only, instead of taking place in separate institutions, this growth and training takes place in the totality of the life of a person.

The embeddedness of our urges in the organic and unreflective spheres of personal life is the reason why the first years of childhood are of such eminent importance for the formation of the whole personality. If grave shocks or frustrations occur in the period of infancy the child has no weapon to fight them. For he has no counteracting or balancing reasoning available; he has no experience and, in addition, he has a strong feeling of dependence. Thus, if childhood, because of its closeness to nature, is an age of particular charm for the sophisticated adult who likes to glorify and sentimentalize it for that reason, it is, on the other hand, an age of extreme exposure. There is no reason to believe that psychic traumata occurring in this period of life can never be healed, but they are certainly very difficult to heal, and often it is the finest kind of personalities who carry the scars with them during their whole life.

Around this inner core of the personality which consists of its vital and natural urges, we may draw a circle indicating a second group; namely, our sensory, manipulative, and loco-motive "abilities." Logically it is doubtful whether we are allowed to place the abilities on the same plane with the vital urges, or with the emotional and intellectual capacities of which we will have to speak later. Whereas it is impossible to clearly localize the capacities just mentioned, the abilities represent physically definable organs for action which we have to use for the realization and satisfaction of our needs. We must be able to perceive, to reach out and grasp, and to move from one place to another in order to come in contact with the object of our desires. Without such abilities our urges would exhaust themselves in a helpless and futile struggle. The evolution of the animal kingdom proves that there is a certain reciprocity of action between urges and abilities; the urges drive the abilities to practice; and the abilities, growing with their exercises, stimulate the urges.

A comparison of different stages of animal life produces another important insight; namely, that man's abilities develop slowly, but are capable of continuous training and achieve, for this very reason, an unusual degree of refinement. Man has been endowed by nature with certain specific characteristics, such as upright posture, stereoscopic vision, prehensile hands, and a nervous system which makes possible a high degree of sensitiveness, innumerable reactions, and speech. The interaction and consistent training of all these and other abilities, such as hearing, taste, smell, and touch allow not only for such top achievements as those of the master craftsman, the virtuoso, or the athlete, but are indispensible requisites for our external and internal culture. Without them we would not live in houses but in caves, and we would not even have a stone ax to cut wood for a warming fire.

While no single capacity of man can be explained without the help of the others, so, also, the development of our abilities cannot be fully understood if we remain within their own orbit. As the driving force behind the abilities there work our vital urges which want to be satisfied; and each of us knows from his own experience that our emotional life, especially our will, sends its impetus constantly into the workshop of the abilities.

But what do we mean when we speak of our emotions and volitions? In our imaginary diagram we would symbolize them by a third circle which swings around the abilities as the abilities swing around the inner circle of the "vital urges."

A whole literature has been written about this question, particularly on the problem as to whether will and emotions represent one and the same function of personality. But a much more radical issue is that of the relationship of our volitional and emotional life to our "vital urges."

Certainly, many of our emotions are nothing but the waves of feeling which accompany our urges in their striving for satisfaction and their attempt at avoiding the opposite. But other emotions are much more complex. We can, for example, become deeply aroused emotionally by the contemplation of a great work of art; subtle and at the same time strong emotions, together with intense will power, are also needed by the composer of a symphony, the writer of a novel, or a scholar who is occupied with the formulation of a system of thought. In addition, we possess the capacity of projecting ourselves into the joys and the sufferings of other people—in other words—the powers of empathy and sympathy. In some way all these emotional experiences are akin to our instinctive life. But they are much more than that.

Let us read together a sonnet by Shakespeare:

The expense of spirit in a waste of shame
Is lust in action; and till action, lust
Is perjur'd, murderous, bloody, full of blame,
Savage, extreme, rude, cruel, not to trust;
Enjoy'd no sooner, but despisèd straight;
Past reason hunted; and no sooner had,
Past reason hated, as a swallow'd bait,
On purpose laid to make the taker mad:
Mad in pursuit, and in possession so;
Had, having, and in quest to have, extreme;
A bliss in proof,—and prov'd, a very woe;
Before, a joy propos'd; behind a dream.
    All this the world well knows; yet none knows well
    To shun the heaven that leads men to this hell.

When we read this sonnet on lust and passion in a con-
genial spirit we are certainly emotionally aroused. But not
because we are in the state of willing something specific;
rather we are in the state of catharsis, or purifying contemplation. We recollect the power of passion we may have felt;
yet, in doing so under the guidance of a poet we acquire perspective—to them and ourselves. In this process we are supported by our "imagination" which not only connects our
own individual existence with the impressions we receive
from reading the sonnet, but which helps us also to learn
from it something about humanity.

Thus that whole mental phenomenon which we call our
emotions, contains three different levels, as it were. On the
first level move such emotions as those which accompany
hunger, feelings, thirst, and sex. Sometimes they can cause a
state of passive and slavish dependence on our bodily desires,
just as they also can create a pleasant feeling of comfort. If
the achievement of a desired object requires perseverance,
the accompanying emotion or complex of emotions is tinged
by will.

But the will which works with and in our emotions can assume a relatively independent role. It may no longer result
from the push of urges, but from motivations that come from

the challenge of goals we would like to reach. Then we have a second level of emotional life, that of primarily volitional character. At this level belong the whole scale of feelings which force the runner to draw the last bit of strength out of his tired body, the soldier to brave the attack of the enemy, and the writer to try the fifth or sixth version of an essay.

At the third and, in a way, highest level have to be placed all those emotions in which mere egotistic desire is dissolved in experiences of universal value. This comes about in religious, intellectual, or esthetic contemplation, or in love that no longer means the lover himself but the beloved object. Through this kind of emotion man elevates himself above his ego. He performs a unique human act which unites him with forces we may call divine, if humility does not forbid us to do so.

But also here we have to refer to the previous statement that no human faculty can feed on itself alone: If somebody becomes absorbed in esthetic contemplation while reading the sonnet by Shakespeare just quoted he not only "feels," but also uses his intellectual faculties, especially his "imagination." In addition, as we said, the sonnet teaches him something about humanity as a whole, for the genius of the great artist raises individual events onto the level of universal validity.

However, the mental function we call "imagination," is only part of a wider group of capacities which we may denote by the general term "intelligence."

Thus we have now in our set of imaginary circles which gradually expand from the urges toward the abilities, and from the abilities toward the emotions, a fourth circle which represents "intelligence." As in the other circles, we are packing different things into one container: namely, "intelligence" in the stricter sense of the word—which is the logical and concept-forming quality, imagination, which is the image-forming quality of the mind, and "intuition," which is the quality of insight or spiritual perception. Without intelligence, imagination runs wild; without imagination, intelligence is sterile; and without intuition—which is the rarest and most sublime mental quality—both intelligence and imagination are denied the discovery of the hidden behind the already revealed verities. Intuition in the most exact sense is "genius," "grace," or *charisma*. It creates; whereas intelligence proper and imagination understand, relate, combine and interpret.

But however great the differences between intelligence, imagination, and intuition, they have one characteristic in common.

If we pass from the inner of our imaginary circles—the urges, through the other circles toward the one representing "intelligence," we shift more and more from the sphere of nature-bound necessity toward a sphere of freedom and differentiation. We could also say, the more we move away from the instinctive toward the primarily mental qualities, the more we arrive at a domain of faculties through which humanity distinguishes itself from animals and also varies greatly within itself. Hunger, thirst, the protective, and the sexual urges we have in common with the beasts of prey in the jungle and the cattle on our farms. Nor do we distinguish widely among ourselves through the urges.

But animals build their nests and shelters, if they build any, always according to certain habits, so that the ornithologist has only to see the form of a nest in order to define the corresponding species of the bird. There is no variation in these patterns and in spite of all skill little individuality except the choice of the locality, and even the latter may be highly determined. But man has developed the art of architecture with its choice and variations; and there is good taste and bad taste according to the esthetic patterns. Man can reflect upon his environment, he can analyze it and abstract from it. However, there are enormous differences between a mathematician occupied with the theory of quanta and relativity, and about forty per cent of the people who are unable to perform the mental operations as demanded in the last two grades of an average American high school. Without this forty per cent, civilization could persist as little as without the inventive genius, though the forty per cent work and grow in relation to the practical tasks of life while abstractions mean little or nothing to them.

But strong individuality and excellence, even though praiseworthy in themselves, must not disturb the interaction of all the different psycho-physical faculties of a person.

In a flower the receptacles are as important as the ovary, the stamens as indispensable as the pistils, and the calyx as necessary as the petals; and they all together are mutually interdependent. So also in the human person no part or function can feed on, or try to separate itself from, the others without endangering the balance and proportions of the whole and creating in an individual a continual state of adolescence, immaturity, or even grave forms of abnormality.

The value which our modern civilization lays especially on intellectual efficiency would be a blessing, if it developed all the other productive faculties of man to the same degree. The fact that it does not is the reason why we have more and more technical achievements and accumulated knowledge, and become at the same time culturally more and more neobarbarians. The dominance of brain power in our civilization creates not only disequilibrium between man's instinctive, emotional, and logical faculties, but also an indigestible diversity of interests and opinions. The differences and isolations become too great to be moored in a common ground of agreement. The result is the centrifugal kind of culture which produces first a sham productivity of constantly changing modes, fads, and thrills; then a harassing feeling of unrest, loneliness, and lack of direction, until suddenly the neglected "herd instinct" in man asserts itself. Then we have all these "intellectuals" who advocate romantic antirationalism and become converted to Catholicism, without ever becoming real Catholics. And in the deserted masses there emerges a violent desire for a "leader" and a protective form of society. Yet historians without deeper insight into the character of man cannot cease wondering why exactly the most individualist and intellectualist nations become collectivist. But rather than being surprising, it is the inevitable link between cause and effect.

The way in which a person integrates his different faculties and qualities into an individual whole gives to his life a particular tenor or flavor. A fugue follows certain laws of harmonics and composition, but within these laws there exists a great variety of musical possibilities. Similarly the human individual develops according to certain laws of human growth and according to personal proclivities which he cannot change arbitrarily without destroying, or at least endangering, the health and rhythm of his life. These proclivities have much to do with his hereditary endowment and his early experiences. But within these limits there exists a variety of personal choices or melodies which are dependent upon a person's opportunity and willingness to develop his capacities as fully as possible.

But human life is too complex to permit a completely harmonious growth of all the different faculties of a person. The elementary forces, inherent in our vital urges, may fight against the demands of our intelligence; our intelligence with its critical and analytical tendency may frustrate our emotions; and our emotions or will may run quicker than our abilities and our intelligence are capable of following. Particularly modern division of labor results easily in the overgrowth of one faculty at the expense of others. Thus we find a considerable number of dangerously one-sided persons among certain professions and vocations which enjoy high social prestige, and are extremely useful from the point of view of technical efficiency. Some people may even prefer one or the other profession, not because of its intrinsic value but because it supports their tendency toward a one-sided development. We have already stated that our modern civilization creates too many persons in whom intelligence bulks out at the expense of their other faculties; consequently they become less and less wise the more they become skilled and learned. Among sportsmen and professional soldiers physical boldness and will power sometimes absorb the finer spheres of emotions and intelligence. What there is left over is a type with little respect for the claims of humanity. Industrial workers have to adjust themselves physically and mentally to ever repeated manipulations which produce a clearly discernible mutation of human physique and behavior. Thus we find some degree of distortion of the harmonious wholeness of human faculties in almost every person. Probably nobody who today wants to be efficient in the pursuit of a purpose can save his personality completely from some kind of twisting and deformation.

III. The Importance of Purpose

On the other hand, it is the close attachment to a definite purpose which enables an individual to become an integrated personality. The process of maturation, which is the molding of an individual into a well-operating whole, must not be understood as resulting from a mere mechanical balance of different faculties. Rather it needs a high degree of motivation to bend all the centrifugal powers in the human personality into a somewhat stable form. And this motivation is impossible without a purpose.

With the inclusion of the concept of purpose into our considerations we now leave the primarily immanent characteristics of human personality. We admit in this way that it is impossible to understand man merely by means of psychology, as this science is generally understood. Instead we have to combine this endeavor with sociological and ethical considerations.

The importance of purpose lies in the fact that no human being can remain within, but must always transcend his ego, in order to find himself. If this process is fluttering and unsteady, without an object or without some combinable objects of loyalty being available, the whole person is bound to be unsteady. The very character of self-transcendence forbids that purposes are merely self-created and egotistic (for then the individual remains too much within himself), or that a purpose is imposed upon him which is inadequate to his own personal talents and inclinations. The result of all such defects would be self-centeredness which can reach grave forms of hysteria, or bitterness and frustration.

No productive life can escape the stately command of duty which sometimes may be combined with hardship and renunciation. But even these unpleasant factors will be accepted by a person who can combine them with an embracing and meaningful purpose. If he is fully motivated, the cumbersome details of the task receive a deeper meaning. Otherwise duty becomes the cool symbol of external tyranny or stifling self-discipline. Many a man has been so subdued by a duty alien to himself that he became insensitive to the joys and responsibilities which make human life full and happy. Thus, in addition to all his misery, he even becomes unproductive.

But it is not only the command of duty, conceived of externally and unaccepted internally, which makes people act against their own inherent destiny. There are many other circumstances which may bring about the same effect: obligations and commitments which, for external or profoundly moral reasons, cannot be broken, or financial considerations in which the crucial issue of survival is involved.

But often it is nothing but the terrific tyranny of convention that forces an individual into the role of a pseudo-self. The sphere on which conventionalism exercises probably its hardest pressure is that of sexual life, for our civilization has been totally unable to resolve the impulsions of sex into the necessary unity of discipline and freedom. The sexual urge, to be sure, is of such power that no culture has managed to lead it into constructive channels without some kind of coercion. But our Western civilization seems to be especially charged with the dynamite of erotic conflict. There is the tradition of Christianity, which under the influence of wrongly understood asceticism has often led men of otherwise highest intelligence and morality to debase all erotic life into the sphere of sin and uncleanliness. There is the obsession with feelings of competition and ownership which do not allow the free development of the partner and are, for this very reason, more liable to create alienation, secrecies, cynicism, and divorces than an atmosphere of freedom and confidence would. There are our late marriages enforced through prolonged professional training and social insecurity. There is the nerve-racking city life and the fatigue from hurry and overwork exactly among the most valuable members of society. There is the fear of having children partly out of merely hedonistic reasons, partly out of economic considerations. And there is finally the emancipation of women which has occurred in a generation not yet ripe to create a fitted social pattern for their new position and all the psychological and economic consequences arising from it.

We are told, furthermore, that about sixty per cent of the total number of beds in American hospitals are occupied by people who suffer from mental diseases or their implications, and that many of these diseases are caused by unsolved sexual problems. The whole situation is aggravated right now by the war with its cruel consequences on the mental health of people and the still more cruel loss of man power which will drive a growing number of women with a profound longing for love and children into conditions difficult to bear in one way or another.

All this will increase into dangerous extremes the number of individuals who are denied the development of their real selves and are forced to accept roles which, like frustrated actors, they do not like to play.

The maladjustment between person and purpose with all its ramifications becomes all the more catastrophic, as it influences not only our conscious, but also, and probably still more, our subconscious life.

Also the "subconscious" is one of the many verbal symbols which the psychologist has to use in order to indicate psychic powers whose working he observes without knowing what they are. Earlier philosophers surmised that forgotten, but potentially retained knowledge sleeps, as it were, under the threshold of the conscious until it is awakened by proper associations. Others denote by the term "subconscious" the whole group of instinctive urges, because they are of unreflective character—more like elemental forces of nature than functions in the service of the rational man. Others believe that in the limbo of the subconscious there meet our frustrated impulses and suppressed fears with certain uncontrollable elements in our hereditary endowment. Still others maintain that our subconscious harbors the primordial fears and myths of the primitive man who still lives with us in our fairy tales, or in our dreams, or in hours when frustration turns over into wild aggressiveness. Certainly our subrational life encompasses a much wider span of experiences than our rational life. Some psychologists believe that ninety per cent of our psychic life is of subconscious character. Probably the analogy is right that our mental existence can be compared with an iceberg, the biggest part of which is always under water.

IV. The Importance of Balance

All the previous considerations touch upon the great problem of human self-control.

Modern man, in his secular and individualistic attitude, has hoped to master himself by dint of his reason, or his will, or by introspection and dissection as evidenced by the various forms of psychoanalysis. Or he believes in work and activity, as such, as means for self-development and inner balance.

All these ideas contain some truth. The emphasis on the rational character of man and his moral will, for example, represents one of the great human ideals since the times of Socrates. However, in spite of the enormous increase of secular enlightenment during the past centuries we have not progressed beyond the times of Pythagoras with regard to the cultivation of the inner personality. On the contrary, we have fewer, if any, men to equal the great spiritual leaders of times bygone.

After all we have found out about the interaction of the diverse capacities of man the reason for this failure can be easily detected. The moment one single capacity claims superiority over the others the result will always be an overt or covert struggle, continual shifting from one extreme toward the other, or false forms of self-habituation with final acceptance of a pseudo-self. But in making himself believe what he actually is not, a person stifles his growth and exposes himself to grave mental and moral danger.

Thus we have to abandon all one-sided schemes of self-control in favor of a more over-all and integrative attitude. What this attitude would be in actuality is not so easy to describe scientifically. So let us try it by means of a simple analogy:—

The act of swimming consists in forgetting to struggle with the water. Only then, can the adept learn how to make regular and successful movements. But the change from the struggling toward the floating is much more psychic than physical; it is an act of confidence which determines the total mental and bodily attitude of the swimmer. It is a sort of autosuggestion which permeates the total man.

Without too much violence to the facts, the analogy from the art of swimming can be transferred to the art of living and of self-control, or whatever name we may prefer. A person can have a life of equilibrium, fearlessness, and natural control of his conscious and subconscious life only if he has achieved a state of mind in which he does not need resort to the artificial effort of one isolated mental power, but in which he is carried by his own self as the good swimmer by the waves and his movements.

To give a person such an attitude of confidential contact with the forces in his person and in life has been the intention of the different devotional precepts recommended by the great religions. They all have pointed at a transcending source of self-control, namely God, who directs our actions, from whom we may receive counsel and strength through prayer and contemplation, and from whom may come reward and punishment. The sacredness of the family, so much emphasized by religion, guarantees in its members, and especially its children, a feeling of protection and belongingness. The rituals which accompany the pious through life, reiterate the divine melody within and behind all individual beings; and through prayer the devout reassert every day their belief in an eternal and protective power.

If the psychological meaning of these precepts becomes translated into nonreligious language it says: Give a person a feeling of security and balance, relate him to purposes and ideas which help him to form embracing loyalties and convictions, and give him the sense of a moral order which he has to recognize not only for the good of others, but for his own good.

And behind all these particular maxims there is a common and deeper one, which says: Forget yourself in something that is greater than you and thus acquire the strength and perspective to harmonize your own existence with the laws and demands of life. Only this attitude will give you the confidence, courage, and discipline without which there is no balance and no self-control.

It has now become evident in this psychological chapter that neither individuals nor societies can thrive without the motivation of purposes and ideas beyond their immediate existence. Some kind of transcendence is indispensable, irrespective of a definite answer to the problem of whether it can spread on the natural and social plane alone, or whether it needs a metaphysical explanation. "Naturalism" too needs a metaphysics in order to be a comprehensive philosophy.

But a somewhat complete understanding of personality compels us not only to include philosophical questions, but ties itself also to the more sociological considerations which we discussed in the first chapter of this book. For with what else did it deal but with the problem of how to enable human beings to find an environment and to lead a life of outer and inner security, confidence and maturity, and thus not only to profit, but also to contribute to their civilization?

One could feel inclined to relate specific qualities of personality to certain of the conditions of civilization such as mentioned in the first part of this book. The opportunities for physical survival and work could be related to the vital urges and abilities; reason to intelligence; faith and love to the emotions; and the claim of excellence to will. But such comparison would bring about the danger of dividing both the totality of civilization, as well as the totality of the human personality into separate departments. As civilization is a whole, so a person is a whole, and either they fit together tolerably as wholes, or the situation will be intolerable.

But if this is true we have to take into account a so-far neglected aspect. Human civilization is not only an environmental and mental phenomenon, but also an historical product, charged with historical dynamic. Hence, in our attempt at arriving at a philosophy of civilization, we must add to the description of its basic social and psychological conditions a brief analysis of those historical forces which work as living elements in our present culture.

CHAPTER III

THE HISTORICAL PERSPECTIVE

I. Introduction—What Is History

The reader may wonder at finding an historical chapter in a book on conditions of civilization and exclaim: Why bother? Let us live in the present! Let us live for the future!

But what is the present? What is the future? In our own individual development the present is but a short breathing spell between what we have done and what we intend to do. But what we intend for today depends on what we did yesterday. And all together depends on the interaction of our personality with our environment. Our personality, however, is largely determined by our dead ancestors, and so is our environment.

Nations and civilizations, in this respect, are not different from personalities. Whenever in the history of mankind, for example, in the French Revolution, a people tried to build a gigantic dam between its future and its past, the waves of the past grew and grew in momentum and finally broke through the artificial barrier. And in our own days the Russian society gradually incorporates some symbols of the past into its pattern, and fights violently against others, which also indicates the existence of the past in the present.

A society is either revolutionary—first inert and then suddenly leaping into unknown regions in order to return later to a half-way point; or it is evolutionary—awake, examining the possibilities of the future in the light of the past, and thus, in the end, arriving at the desired goal in about the same time without so much destruction and bloodshed as is generally connected with revolutions.

History involves individuals too. When a snowball gets rolling we may stand by and watch with pleasure and apprehension. But if it heads for something breakable we run to interfere before the momentum of its rolling is too strong and rapid. Our part in history is similar.

We stop or start events and trends in our everyday world, which is our history, according to our knowledge of their character and composition.

The individual's responsibility, then, is to know the past in order to use it for the present. Only when he acts may he also enjoy contemplation of the great panorama we call history.

Hence, we need a good deal of historical consciousness and conscience in attempting to find, or to build up, the basic social and psychological conditions which are requisite for the development of a sound civilization.

If we first take stock and try to find out what the storage of our civilization contains as promise for the future, the answer can only be divided.

Against an unheard of wealth of potentialities, accumulated in a long history of material and cultural progress, stands a similarly unheard of mass of unsolved contrasts. The gigantic enterprise of modern man to change a world of universal authority into a world of individual independence has, in many ways, surpassed his capacity. The experimental attitude we are so proud of leads every day to new discoveries and inventions, but it also throws modern man into a continual state of restlessness with deceptive desires and ambitions. Our intellectual and emotional reactions to the problems of life run the whole gamut of possible guesses: from idealism to materialism, from orthodoxy to skepticism, from rationalism to romanticism, from atheism to obscurantist substitute religions, and from extreme self-assertion to doubt and despair.

Such a wealth of speculation can be a sign of health and

creativeness if counterbalanced by sound social relationships. But at present, economic and national competitions have created dangerous class cleavages and thrown both rich and poor, victors and defeated into a continual state of insecurity. Thus the enormous increase in intellectuality and external wealth has failed to lead toward a similar degree of mental maturity and actual human welfare. We are bewildered because our immediate purposes, however simple or complicated, egotistic or sacrificial, are no longer hinged to great common and uniting purposes which would show us and our nation a place in the process and progress of human history.

In our political propaganda and in schools we constantly repeat such great words as freedom and humanity, but sometimes they sound to us like dying echoes of the past. We certainly believe in their value; we even defend them against willful destroyers, but too often in our own ranks we see them used in charters and manifestoes merely for propaganda purposes. And because they are not meant seriously, while at the same time they appeal to the highest moral impulses in man, they are bound to create disillusion on all sides.

There is now a general anxiety among the best men in the democracies that both the task of democracy and the task of peace may be too difficult. We are afraid that the European continent which for more than two thousand years was the central source of Western civilization may have lost its regenerative power. And the worst of all is that we do not know who could take up its heritage.

But what is this heritage?

II. THE THREE COMPONENTS OF WESTERN CIVILIZATION

One can blame Western civilization for almost all defects the human mind can imagine. One can even say that it is built on a tradition of ideals which never became realized. But one fault this civilization certainly did not have was lack of inner vitality. Rather there was an abundance of productivity, tension, and continual change. No idea could come to light without being contradicted; no power could exert itself without being attacked; no attempt at unity could be made without being doubted.

Western civilization resembles a highly talented man, in whom the gifts of genius dwell together with defects characteristic of the abnormal, in whom exuberant hopes and rapid progress alternate with periods of depression; and in whom the wonderful urge toward sympathy and creation is often endangered by the neurotic menace of the death instinct and by the sinister lust of brutality.

And the friends and physicians who love and admire this man without being able to help him wonder whether this kind of personality may not result from a combination of hereditary components which can produce a wealth of great ideas and actions when reconciled, but which can just as well cause breakdown and disaster when they refuse to co-operate.

What are now at least the main hereditary, or historical, components which have rendered Western civilization both so rich and so defective?

They are first the legacy from Greek-Roman Antiquity, second the legacy from Christianity, and third the legacy of the Teutonic element.

In the seething crucible, which was Europe at the end of Antiquity, the disintegrating Western nations of the Roman Empire were melted with the Teutonic tribes which swept from the steppes of present Russia westward over almost the whole continent. The melting never became perfect; still today we can distinguish the elements of which the new product was composed.

A. *The Greek Spirit of Rationality*

One of these elements—as has already been said—was the Greek civilization. In the primitive encyclopedias which the few educated clergymen read in the dawn of the Middle Ages there can be found the vestiges of Pythagorean, Platonic, Aristotelian, and Stoic philosophies; traces of Ciceronian humanism, and remainders of Euclidian and Ptolemaic mathematics which the learned theologians used for fixing the dates of the Christian calendar. The Franks and the other nations which had settled during the sixth and seventh centuries accepted also parts of Roman law and administration which often stood as rather alien elements beside Teutonic legal customs.

But medieval man received from Antiquity not only this or that particular element of knowledge, conduct, or government; more important than all details was the mental training they acquired from their acquaintance with ancient thought. The unforgettable quality of the Greek mind is its urge toward rationality. The eternal contributions of Greek civilization are in intellectual method and vocabulary capable of ordering the world by dint of logical concepts and categories. It took a long time, up to the eleventh century, before medieval man learned to use the methods of thinking, as Aristotle had worked them out, for abstracting ideas in systematic fashion. But when once he had grasped it there was an outburst in intellectual creativeness. It had its culmination in the theological system of Thomas Aquinas which represents still today the canonical philosophy of the Catholic Church.

B. *The Spirit of Christianity*

The strange fact that we find the great pagan Aristotle suddenly in the twilight of a Christian cathedral was due to the existence of a divine revelation of more sacred character than even the wisdom of the ancients. This revelation was supposed to have come directly from God, the Creator, and His Son, whom He had sent to earth in order to save sinful men from eternal damnation. Thus we have beside the Greek intellectual legacy, as the second component in our civilization, the Christian religion. When this religion, in the fourth and fifth centuries, became generally accepted, it was, however, no longer of pure character, but had been considerably modified by its contact with Greek philosophy. The Nicene Creed of the Church was the result of an ardent struggle between different Christian schools, all influenced by Greek philosophies, particularly about the identity of the nature of Christ and the nature of God. As a matter of fact, the acceptance of the Nicene Creed in 325 was a diplomatic subterfuge proposed by the emperor Constantine in order to secure peace within the Church and through it within his empire. Though a compromise, the Nicene Creed involved a considerable change of the prevailing Christian tradition according to which Christ was not God's equal.

The medieval theologians when reading the first verses of the Gospel according to Saint John concerning the identity between the Word and God did not realize that they had before them a mixture of the Jewish idea of Jehovah and the Neoplatonic idea of the *Logos*. The great bridge-builder between the Jewish-Christian and the Western tradition had been Saint Paul whose missionary activities in Greece we find described in Acts XVII:

> Then certain philosophers of the Epicureans, and of the Stoics, encountered him. And some said, What will this babbler say? others said, He seemeth to be a setter forth of strange gods: because he preached unto them Jesus, and the resurrection. . . . Then Paul stood in the midst of Märs' hill, and said, Ye men of Athens, I perceive that in all things ye are too superstitious. For as I passed by, and beheld your devotions, I found an altar with this inscription, TO THE UNKNOWN GOD. Whom therefore ye ignorantly worship, him declare I unto you. God that made the world and all things therein, seeing that he is Lord of heaven and earth, dwelleth not in temples made with hands; . . .

C. *The Teutonic Element*

With the migration of the nations a new and third tributary flew into the stream of Western civilization, the Teutonic element. We are accustomed to describe it as "barbaric" in comparison with the Greek-Roman civilization. Barbaric it was, if we have in mind the onslaught of warrior tribes driven by internal pressures from Asia and eastern Europe into the realms of the Roman Empire, if we think of the slaughter of men and the sacking of cities as described by historians and Church fathers.

Yet, there must have been a goodly portion not only of physical, but also of mental vitality in these Teutonic hordes. As most migrating peoples they seemingly possessed a high degree of collective discipline mixed with democratic forms of council and self-administration; they possessed a well-developed ritual and imaginative form of polytheism; there were artists among them with an amazing power of expressing their mystic yearning in strange geometrical forms. Finally, the strategical and organizational talent of the invaders, as well as their social adaptability, was great enough to induce the ruling classes of the Roman Empire as early as in the second century after Christ to appoint Germans from the borderlines of the Empire as officers in the army. They married the daughters of influential families and rose into the nobility. When in the fifth and sixth centuries after Christ, the Roman Empire, except for the Byzantine part, fell to pieces, many of these Teutonic newcomers had already adopted Roman customs, luxury, and administration.

Since then three main streams of our Western civilization flow together: one coming from Greece and Rome, the second coming from Mount Sinai and the towns of Palestine, and the third from the steppes and the great rivers of eastern Europe.

But have these three streams really flowed into one? Sometimes we may think so. There exists something we may call a European civilization, and those who have breathed its depth and charm are united by this experience in spite of all inner national conflicts and suicidal wars among the peoples of Europe. On the other hand, again and again it has become clear that Europe was not wide and strong enough to merge the waters of the three tributaries into one steadily flowing river. Perhaps no civilization would have the power to unite such contrasts.

D. *The Contrasts*

But why—we may ask in somewhat more detail—are the three components of Western culture so contrastable and so incompatible with each other?

The Greek spirit was pagan not only because the Greeks lived before Christ but because their particular creativeness issued from a situation in which the official religion, for the intelligent people, was much more lore and ceremony than a universal answer to profound inner concerns. Thus, the educated Greeks had to use philosophy in order to satisfy their desire for a comprehensive view of life. No doubt, they included much of a religious metaphysics in their philosophical thought which was always open to new suggestions. But it was man made, not revealed. For them there never had been a Moses to whom God appeared and said (Exodus III, 14):

"I AM THAT I AM; ... Thus shalt thou say unto the children of Israel, I AM hath sent me unto you."

Consequently there was no other criterion among the Greeks than human measures and human effort, however deep and grand. When they called something good and true, they did so, not because God had approved of it, but because they had found that it was effective and in harmony with the laws of the universe.

The Jews believed that man was driven from Paradise because he had followed the advice of the serpent and eaten the fruit which opened his eyes and helped him to "be as gods, knowing good and evil." But this eating from the tree of wisdom was exactly what the Greeks considered the highest virtue of man. Plato's ideal state was one led by wise men in possession of the art of dialectics. While the Jews had the Prophets, the Greeks had the great philosophers, logicians and artists; they established the pattern of culture even for the conquering Romans though the latter were superior to the Greeks in the art of administration, and in jurisprudence.

When the first Christian communities appeared within this pagan world they were despised as human trash shunning the light of day and meeting at night in strange conventicles. However, as all newcomers who want to survive in a powerful environment, they adjusted themselves intellectually and socially. When Constantine the Great recognized Christianity as the religious foundation on which to build up his empire the bishops were powerful men and, in addition, the amalgamation between Christian supernaturalism and Greek philosophy had been completed.

But could it really be completed? Was not the Christian faith as alien an element within Greek thought, as the Christian Church was originally an alien element within the Roman Empire? The center of ancient morality is a manly and noble form of self-assertion, whereas the center of the Christian Gospel is love and humility. In all decisive situations of life the two are bound to contradict each other. As the whole history of our Western civilization proves, they can be reconciled only on the surface. There have been saints, even heroic saints, or great statesmen and warriors. But when the saint, as sometimes happened, began to mingle in the affairs of European society, his saintliness was generally lost. And when the statesman, or warrior listened too willingly to the voice of love and sympathy within his soul, he ruined his cause because in the reckless struggle for survival in war and diplomacy the morally best man is, according to the rules of this game, generally not the fittest and most successful. Ethically, he is right, but his opponent will take advantage of him.

The conflict of these two principles in life, namely love and self-assertion, appears also in European education. The secular knowledge taught in the schools of the ancient and medieval Church was more or less the one transmitted from the pagan curriculum; no serious attempt was made at an intrinsic unification of the Aristotelian and the Christian concepts of life in the *Septem artes liberales*. And however much the classical schools of Europe professed to unite Christian *pietas* with ancient ideals, the young aristocrats learned the art of living and ruling from the biographies of great statesmen and warriors in Plutarch's *Parallel Lives* rather than from the Sermon on the Mount. Theoretically they learned in their religious instruction that love is a greater force than diplomacy or power, but only few ventured to test this hypothesis.

The influx of the third constituent element in our Western civilization, the Teutonic, could only strengthen the contrast between the self-assertive Greek and the sacrificial Christian spirit. Accustomed to the hard life of warriors and hunters, living with a folklore and a code of honor which glorified the hero and despised the meek, and being at the same time strong individualists despite a certain tribal collectivism, these Teutonic peoples founded a highly militant society. It is touching to observe the embarrassment with which the author of the Old High German epic the *Heljand* tries to reconcile his audience with the martyrdom of Christ. The profound heroism which lies in this martyrdom as in every principle of nonviolence was not understood by the poet. Instead he adapts Jesus as much as possible to the ideals of a Germanic hero and dwells, beyond all due proportion, on the story of Saint Peter drawing his sword and cutting off the ear of one of the servants of the High Priest.

Only in one respect certain Teutonic groups displayed a profound affinity to the Jewish-Christian tradition; they had a strong contemplative tendency which drove them to use the Christian doctrine as the starting ground for profound mystical speculation. Thus arose, out of medieval scholastic philosophy, Master Eckart's and Nicolaus Cusanus' mystical ideas and, out of post-Renaissance humanism, the theosophical systems of Leibnitz and Schelling. The Gothic cathedrals of the Middle Ages are but the architectural symbols of this mystical trend. The Catholic church, built partly on mystical transcendentalism and partly on Greek-Latin logic and institutionalism, has, up to this date, not been capable of reconciling this contrast within its own theology. And this very defect has kept it alive.

It is the grandeur, and at the same time the failure of medieval man that he, in contrast to the disillusioned modern mind, believed in the possibility of harmonizing the contrasts in his civilization by means of three great universal ideas, each of them comprehensive in itself and at the same time supposed to blend with the others.

The first of these three ideas was that of the Holy Roman Empire. Charles the Great and his successors were held to be the heirs of the Roman emperors and to symbolize the political unity of the Christian world. This idea caused more war than peace and more harm than good both to the Italian nation, the seat of the old Roman caesars, and particularly to the German nation which had the doubtful honor of harboring the new emperors. Of the three universal ideas of the Middle Ages the idea of the political unity of mankind was the least effective though it represented a dream great enough to inspire mankind at least up to the sixteenth century.

The second universal idea was that of the Catholic church with the Holy See as its symbol. As the emperors were believed to be the successors of the caesars, so the popes were believed to be the successors of Christ and Saint Peter. Also the idea of the Christian catholicity of Europe was never fully realized; large parts of the Christian world, especially the Greek Orthodox church, remained outside papal influence, and the reign of some of the greatest popes is less a part of the history of human love than of shrewd diplomacy and suppression. Nevertheless, whereas the dream of European political unity under the successors of the caesars is gone, large groups of the Western civilization still see the center of spiritual authority in Rome.

The third universal idea which united the scholars of the Middle Ages was the community of language through the acceptance of Latin as the medium of communication in the fields of learning and diplomacy. This community made possible learning from the same standard books, an exchange of students and teachers all over the Christian world, and the proud feeling of belonging to the great supernatural republic of erudite men. Latin transmitted to the Teutonic nations the vocabulary of a highly trained civilization. The logical virtuosity and the flexibility of this language made it possible for the medieval philosophers to erect the first systems of Christian thought and to concentrate, in this way, the speculative powers of medieval man toward high and lofty goals. But Latin, for the medieval man, was not only a mere instrument of learning and communication; it represented for him the glory and authority of Antiquity which he admired as at the central period of all history, past and future, and as at the common source of civilization. Latin symbolized the intellectual unity of mankind, as the Church and the imperium symbolized its religious and political oneness.

To be sure this universal idea was of very limited character. Not more than a portion of one per cent of the population used this medium of internationality, understood the ideas it dealt with, and felt themselves members of an international commonwealth of minds. Nor must one suppose that the religious and cultural aspirations of the intellectual group radiated deeply into the minds of the average man, or even of the secular aristocracy.

The original sources describing the life of medieval man prove that he, like us, suffered from spiritual discord and civil strife. He was cruel, untamed, and superstitious; if he had had our modern weapons of destruction, he would have used them as recklessly as we do at present. But a few, at least, were profoundly inspired by the ideal of divine unity of mankind, and—the important point—they were acknowledged as the spiritual leaders of mankind.

III. The Rising Forces of Modernity

In the course of the fourteenth century the disintegration of medievalism began as the result of social and spiritual factors which, so to speak, form a second layer of components in the genesis of Western civilization. The primitive medieval system of barter gave way to the modern money exchange system. As any fundamental change in the economic order, these first signs of a capitalistic order appeared not without grave convulsions. The feudal system, with the emperor at the top of the secular hierarchy, could no longer enforce the obedience of the great vassals of Europe who felt themselves more and more as princes of sovereign nations. Even within each rising nation the feudal order with its innumerable guilds, corporations, and complicated interdependencies became too clumsy to respond to the needs of the new, more centralized governments.

In addition, the rising national self-consciousness drew into its orbit more and more of the social and spiritual ideals of the people. Medieval philosophers such as Hugh of St. Victor and Vincent of Beauvais had written: "Weak is the man who feels himself bound to one country. Stronger is he who is at home in several countries; but blessed is he who considers the whole world a place of exile." In contrast, the new humanist educators praise the patriotic duties, recommend to the younger generation to fight for the glory of their family and for their own prestige, and develop a strong sense for the ethical and esthetic value of individuality. In all fields of life the medieval attitude of Dante represents the state of the transition. In one respect his *Divine Comedy* is the consummation of the religious thought of medieval Christianity. In other respects it breaks through its boundaries. It is highly individualistic despite its orthodoxy, and it is written in Italian, not Latin. From then on we see the young trees of native poetry and thought overgrowing the old tree of Latin literature. Whenever people wish to express their most personal religious, political, or erotic emotions, they decide, with a few exceptions, in favor of the language of their heart, against the language of their brain. Not even the efforts of the humanist poets succeed in regaining ground for the language of Virgil and Horace. Invariably they were condemned to artificiality. Only in the cool sphere of scholarly and philosophical abstraction did Latin remain dominant up to the seventeenth century.

There still remained the Roman church as the last fortress of European catholicity, but it was too undermined by dissension and corruption within its own garrison. More and more sects wanted a return to original Christianity and a more personal relation to God without the unnecessary paraphernalia of magic institutionalism. The new absolutist governments felt themselves strong enough to protest against the supremacy of both the emperor and the pope and to risk even the threats of excommunication and the Inquisition.

But the most serious problem for the Church arose from a new conception of truth and the methods of arriving at it. Even within the scholastic philosophy of the thirteenth and fourteenth centuries the struggle never abated over the justification of a two-fold verity: one being divine and springing from the revelation, the other being natural and springing from man's own thinking. Yet, this conflict was still medieval. The real break occurred or, one could also say, the modern era began with the rise of the empirical scientific method. Instead of scholastic theology a new universal form of thought and language became introduced, one of greater importance than any other single language ever possessed by mankind, namely, the language of numbers. Though number concepts differ from the concepts of ordinary communicative language, what else are they but symbols of man's capacity to subordinate the fortuities of nature to the concept of an orderly universe?

The development of mathematical language became possible after the introduction of the Hindu-Arabic number system in the twelfth century after Christ. But not before it was used for the analysis and description of empirical observations in the Renaissance did it turn out to be the powerful instrument through which the modern mind freed itself from the primarily deductive methods of medieval scholastic Aristotelianism.

Protestant historians have been inclined to connect the beginning of the modern individualist era with the religious movement of the Reformation. Truly, Luther and Calvin emphasized the necessity of personal religious experience in the process of salvation. Thus they related the person more directly to God and broke medieval hierarchical feudalism in the realm of religion. In consequence of his greater individualism the educated Protestant became inclined to venture more freely toward new intellectual horizons. Also, the democratic idea of the Natural Rights of Man, as laid down in the American Declaration of Independence, was molded under Protestant influence, though historically it is of Greek-Roman and Christian ancestry. But these facts must not induce us to think that the religious leaders of the Reformation were scientifically more enlightened than the Catholic hierarchy. On the contrary, in the times of the Renaissance the latter harbored a considerable number of men who in consequence of their liberality were an offense to the religious radicalism of the Protestants.

If Protestant theologians like to attribute the rise of modernity to changes in the religious attitude, or other historians to economic or political modifications, with just as much or even more justification a scientist could maintain that the dawn of the modern mind began in consequence of the more ingenious application of numerical symbols and exact observations. Through them man discovered that his planet was no longer the center of the universe; through them he also learned the art of explaining life in terms of cause and effect. And these are perhaps the most important phases in the shift from medievalism toward modernity.

To what degree has this process of enlightenment permeated our total civilization?

In spite of the centuries which have elapsed since the times of Luther and Galileo we are still in the conflict between medievalism and modernity. Much though we have progressed in the theoretical and applied sciences, in our social and political thinking we still live in a primarily prescientific, emotional, and egotistic attitude. In medieval times the earth was the center of the universe, and this was certainly an error. However, today for many people the center of the universe is they themselves, or their business and economic system, or their nation, each of them being much smaller in spiritual horizon than the earth was for a scholastic philosopher. No integrating philosophy allows modern man to see knowledge and action, his personal and political life in an embracing and inspiring whole. In a radical sense of the word, we are still in a state of precivilization in which fear and superstition so easily prevail over the rational qualities of man.

IV. THE PROBLEMS OF MODERNITY

A. *Rationalism and Science*

Since, in the times of the Renaissance, the failure of the medieval attempt at cultural conformity became evident, Western man has lived in an atmosphere of unceasing spiritual adventure. As early as the fifteenth and sixteenth centuries there appear new cosmologies which repeat on a higher level of knowledge the attempts of the early Greek philosophers at explaining the universe as a systematic enterprise on a grand scale. Later, in the period of Enlightenment, Locke, Hume and their followers probe into the qualities of human reason in order to judge its validity; finally, Kant elaborates the first comprehensive system of thought in which reason acquires full critical perspective about itself and its relation to its great mental rival, faith. Kant was indebted to the empiricism of Locke and Hume, but he was indebted also to the rationalism of Descartes.

From Descartes' resolve to escape the claws of doubt through reliance on unpremised thinking, still more than from Locke and Hume, the European intellect drew the courage of radical questioning and, at the same time, the conviction that such questioning leads either to faith in a profound contact between the human mind and reality, or to complete relativism and the insanity of utter loneliness.

Descartes and the other builders of rationalist systems of thought decided for the faithful form of rationalism which reached its climax in the idealism of the German philosopher Hegel. This system interprets the history of mankind as the result of the continual self-evolution of the Spirit. Thus it represents an attempt at a synthesis between the Greek idea of *Logos*, as the ordering principle of the world, the Christian-Augustinian idea of the final end of history in the Kingdom of God, and the mystical conception of evolution. Hegel, as every great post-Kantian philosopher to a degree, was a disciple of Kant. Yet, the very central achievement of Kant's methodological prudence; namely, the careful distinction between the competences of reason and faith, he did not respect. For it is the greatness, as well as the weakness, of Hegel's system that for him the human mind was so deeply embedded in divine reason that every new step in the self-interpretation of this human mind could lead only toward a deeper understanding of the Divine Essence. Thus the combination of rationality and piety which is so characteristic of the age of Enlightenment, developed in Hegel to full flower.

No doubt, such a philosophical synthesis is one of abundant confidence. Hegel was sure that, through his dialectical combination of subjective reason which works in man, of objective reason which works in history and institutions, and of absolute reason which works in God, he had integrated the great components of philosophical thought into one coherent whole. He was also convinced that he had provided for future generations of thinkers the final structure into which to build the changing details of expanding knowledge.

But not for a long time is man allowed to sit at the table of the gods. If some do, others mind it; not necessarily out of envy, but also out of humility and a profound feeling of the frightening exposure of all *creatura creata* to sin and error.

Thus Hegel and the whole rationalist movement, which had started so proudly in the Renaissance, were bound to find their opponents. The most incisive among them were the pessimist Schopenhauer in the philosophical, and the mystic Kierkegaard in the religious camps. Schopenhauer stressed the difference between will or instinct on the one hand and reason on the other. Kierkegaard, taking up, as it were, the Kantian scheme of criticism on the theological plane, emphasized the dualism between knowledge and faith, the anxiety of all human existence and its consequent need for salvation through faith in Divine Grace. He died in 1855, and in the following decades of Victorian prosperity and scientific cocksureness only a few knew his work. He is one of the thinkers to whom people do not listen before a crisis has thrown them out of their complacency. No wonder that Kierkegaard's influence spread from his native country Denmark first over to the seething climate of Germany, and only now over to England and America, for here also the foundations of the liberal era have begun to rock materially and ideologically.

But there arose still another opposition against rationalist idealism. The natural scientists, who at the beginning of the nineteenth century entered a new stage of methodical research, rebelled against the arrogance of an unempirical and deductive sort of philosophy. They could prove that this kind of abstract speculation forced nature into its preconceived concepts rather than modestly listening to what it had to tell. The same was true with regard to the Romantic philosophies which under the influence of Schelling spread over the continent.

The American scientist Louis Agassiz—to mention only one among many—wrote in the second half of the nineteenth century:

With the school of the [Romantic] physiophilosophers began (at least in our day and generation) that overbearing confidence in the abstract conceptions of the human mind as applied to the study of nature, which still impairs the fairness of our classifications, and prevents them from interpreting truly the natural relations binding together all living beings.[1]

In contradiction to this philosophical apriorism he stated: "A physical fact is as sacred as a moral principle; our own nature demands for us this double allegiance."

The deplorable collision between philosophy and science in the nineteenth century has resulted in a general suspicion of speculative synthesis from which not only the philosophers but higher learning as a whole have suffered greatly. We may have become accurate in details, but we certainly are ignorant and indifferent with respect to the meaning of life as a whole.

Yet, there is, perhaps, one hope for a resurgence of philosophy. It may come from the scientists themselves. In their search for the deeper principles and unity of nature they are increasingly compelled to subject their work to thorough philosophical examination and, at the same time, to have resort to metaphysical ideas which they have shunned so far. With science being so much in the center of interest this give and take of ideas between two former opponents may start a new era of thought.

Unfortunately, the split between the philosophical tradition and the modern attitude has been widened by modern industry, which is the result of the application of specialized scientific research to mass production.

Practically, this form of industry began in the manufacturing cities of Italy and the Netherlands at the dawn of our modern era. But it did not change the life of Western society considerably before the invention of the steam engine and the use of electricity. The majority of the Western people in the period of George Washington still worked with technical tools more similar to those of the Greeks in the times of Pericles than to those used in modern scientific industry and

[1] For this and the quotation following see the article by W. E. Byles, "Louis Agassiz, Philosopher," *Harvard Educational Review*, Vol. XII, 1942, pp. 181-193.

agriculture. The rapid process of industrialization has not only paved completely new ways for the discovery and utilization of the resources of this earth and created untold comforts; it has also revolutionized our social and political structure to such a degree that the mastery over nature of which modern man is so proud has been more than offset by his bewilderment in the face of the great economic and social problems of the Industrial Civilization. With this bewilderment coincides his loss of the traditional spiritual resources. For one of the results of modern industrialization is the vanishing of genuine religion in our city population which through its press, financial power, and concentration of the political machinery determines so decidedly the destiny of whole nations. Our city dwellers live in a man-made world; sunrise and sunset do not color their days; they do not sense the sowing, the growth, the perils, and the harvesting of the crop; the great decisions in their lives are made by men, dependent on men, changed by men. Under such conditions the sense for the metaphysical background of life disappears easily. Instead of profound reverences nothing is left but perhaps a decent, though spiritually anemic humanitarianism. And often there opens a spiritual vacuum into which can creep prejudices, worse or certainly not better than those of earlier times.

But why did religion fail to cope with the challenges of the technical age?

B. *The Role of Religion in Modern Society*

In the rivalry between speculation and science as it began at the end of the Middle Ages, theology as well as rational philosophy has fallen short. Unfortunately, but inevitably, it has drawn into its defeat even religion as such. Who would have thought so in the times of the Protestant reformations when men fought and died for their religious convictions? But after the first decades of excitement, Protestantism as a church and a theological system did not escape the common plight of established religion; namely, reaction and timidity. As a whole, Protestantism failed to see the great opportunities inherent in the sciences for its own enrichment; it also failed, as all groups in a continual defense attitude, to be creative in its own domain. Instead of the dynamic courage of a Luther and a Calvin, the Protestant theologians preferred a sterile orthodoxy, and when in the eighteenth and nineteenth centuries "liberal" or "critical" theology developed it was much more a phase of general scholarly enlightenment than of an inner religious reform. Only the different forms of Pietism saved Protestantism from utter sterility. Even more than the Protestant churches, the Catholic church proved its attitude of conservatism; the Vatican Council in Rome, to the disappointment of many of the best Catholics, declared on October 20, 1870 the infallibility of the pope when he speaks *ex cathedra*. It also declared, through an Encyclical of Leo XIII in 1879, *Aeterni Patris* the teachings of Thomas Aquinas (who lived from 1225–1274) to be the basis of the Catholic theology.

There is now, without any doubt, a revival of both Catholicism and Protestantism, in spite, or perhaps, in consequence of their dangerous exposure to secularization and abuse by political powers. One impetus in this revival tends to connect religion more closely with the urgent social and political problems of the present, the other springs from a new consciousness of the transcendant sources of salvation, and at some places the two streams begin to flow together. However, it remains to be seen whether these new movements will produce theologians of the quality of true reformers.

Yet, it is not only the theologians who determine the role of religion in history. The German Reformation and the Calvinism of Geneva, Holland, and England were not only religious events, but accompanied by political, economic, and educational revolutions.

Is it a mere caprice of history, or merely a result of political constellations, that after some decades of sweeping victories all over Europe, the Protestant Reformation became confined to the Germanic countries? Or has it a deeper significance? Does it express a definite discrepancy between the Latin and the Germanic mentalities—even in religion—though both have accepted the same, originally foreign, Jewish-Christian creed?

This problem has lured some historians into speculations about national and ethnic characters of rather romantic quality, for nobody will ever be able to decide to what degree variations in the behavior of nations are due to genuine or "innate" differences, or to environmental conditions. In addition, with respect to religions no one knows to what degree a religion forms the people, or a people the religion.

However, one fact seems to be clear enough to permit some definite statement. The Catholic church, in consequence of its strongly centralized and supernational hierarchical structure, and in consequence of its dogma concerning the sacredness of individual property, will offer a stronger opposition against the modern trends toward socialism than the Protestant churches which, in addition to their many divisions, are rather dependent on national governments. Even in Catholic countries the process of secularization may already have advanced so far that politics has its own momentum. But should this not be true then the faithful Catholics would in the future, as in the past, represent an element more strongly opposed to political and economic changes than the Protestants. In case of political crises this could mean a continuation or even increase of the unfortunate split between Catholics and Protestants on the political level. And since, in our times, political fanaticism is not less intensive than the religious fanaticism of earlier centuries, the conflict may be as cruel as any Inquisition ever was, as the recent history of Spain has proved sufficiently.

C. *The Modern State*

It would now be tempting for a systematic mind to take into account the bearing of the third component of medieval civilization, which we called the Teutonic, on modern civilization. But such a discussion would of necessity be artificial for two reasons. What we call "the modern Western civilization" is due to the contributions of, and cultural cross-fertilizations among Latin, Teutonic, and Slavic elements. Nor can one say that after the settlement of the modern state systems, in most of which a particular ethnic group prevails, the Teutonic element has always been in a leading or aggressive role. Rather with the two recent World Wars it has become involved in a fratricidal conflict which may mark the beginning of its gradual displacement by other ethnic groups.

Thus the factor which, in addition to rational thought and religion, has molded modern civilization most decidedly, can no longer be sought in a specific ethnic element. It is the modern state.

During the past centuries the state has become the most embracing and powerful of all social institutions. The democratic citizen of today indulges in the feeling that he has achieved a higher degree of political influence than men of previous ages, with the exception perhaps of the Athenians under Pericles and the Romans in their Republican period. But in all likelihood the feudal society of the Middle Ages gave its free men more opportunity to share in the life of their community than we generally believe. They were even forced by circumstances to do so. Whereas many of us think we have done our duty in casting our vote, the medieval citizen had to serve in his guild, in military and communal corporations, and in religious and social associations, all of which bound him closely together with his fellow men. The medieval organization of society did not break down because there was too little chance for activity. It broke down because it was too complicated and cumbersome for quick action on a large scale, and because the considerable amount of self-administration in the different units allowed too much room for corruption, coterie, friction among parties, and warfare among vassals.

The rise of central absolutist governments during the

transition period from medievalism to our modern time is largely due to the support of the active and progressive middle classes. They needed a more effective organization of governmental control for carrying through their expanding business with a higher degree of security than was feasible in a continual state of fight between cities and cities, vassals and vassals, merchants and knightly waylayers. The merchants were interested in good highways, in sound legal procedure, and in a better secular education for their children. On the whole, absolutism was a historically necessary step from medieval regionalism toward modern planning on a larger scale. And the breakdown of the same absolutism in modern times was due much less to its organizational pattern as such than to its compromising with the older, still powerful leagues of the feudal nobility and the clergy. They built a cordon of courtiers and parasites around the monarch, isolated him from his people and gave him the feeling of a superhuman, almost Godlike being. They got hold of the tax system, insisted on the separation of social classes, and established in this way new feudal privileges, different from the ones they had lost during their fight against the rising monarchical power at the end of the Middle Ages, but of equal profit.

Under the pressure of these disappointing experiences the citizens, who first had supported absolutism, abandoned it. The French Revolution unfolded the banner of liberty, equality, and fraternity. Under the spell of these words we are inclined to conceive of the revolt of the citizens of Paris against their King as a great act of liberation from governmental fetters. In a sense this is true. But the moment we inspect the situation more carefully, we arrive at a paradoxical result. The absolutism of the kings and the privileges of nobility and clergy were abolished, but the power of the state increased despite—or should one better say, by virtue of?—democracy. For the modern citizen, complacently considering the state his own creation, and at the same time faced with an increasing complexity of social and political responsibilities, has been rather inclined to shift the burden from his own shoulders to the government. The French regime in the times of Louis XIV to Louis XVI had no responsibility for education; the church took care of it. It had little responsibility for public welfare; religious associations or the communities had to feed the poor. The French government did much less for transportation than a modern government does. There were still a large number of rather independent guilds of merchants, artisans and professional workers. The power of absolutism was in the army, the legal courts, the control of vocational mobility, and the taxation.

This was exactly the kind of interference which the wealthier middle classes with their expanding desire for independent enterprise resented more than anything else. Thus their practical desires coincided with the gospel of freedom heralded by the great liberals of the seventeenth and the eighteenth centuries, though these men did not mean freedom of business, but freedom of the individual and his conscience or, in other words, the full establishment of the natural rights of man. The fusion of genuine liberalism and the capitalist idea of uncontrolled enterprise—though natural and inevitable—was one of the greatest catastrophies in modern history. Because in this way the liberal tradition, stemming from the best of Greek and Christian thought and concerned with humanity as a whole, could, in the minds of the people, become identified with the economic doctrine of *laissez faire, laissez aller* with thinkers as Adam Smith, Jeremy Bentham, John Stuart Mill, and Herbert Spencer as not always fairly used sponsors. However, when people profit from an idea they do not insist on logical subtleties. The liberal bourgeoisie of the nineteenth century also refused to see the deplorable conditions among the working classes who had nothing to offer and sell but their physical strength and skill.

When finally in the big industrial centers misery, injustice, and delinquency became too appalling; when old farming districts became depopulated; and when revolutions threatened the peace of business and "the march of progress," advocates of economic liberalism were both unwilling and incapable of coping with these social dangers. They left the responsibility for public welfare, education of the masses, and even of economic planning largely to the government, at the same time resenting the social consequences of this. Even the executives of the big cartels which in the course of the last decades have swallowed up more and more of the smaller entrepreneurs were in periods of depression forced to call on the government for subsidies. For only in this way of compromise could the so-called free society and some kind of free enterprise be salvaged from the revolution of desperate masses. The Franklin D. Roosevelt administration in the United States is an example of the situation just described.

Economically influentianal groups in democratic countries still explain the increase in central planning as a kind of free deal with the government. This is, as a matter of fact, wrong, for in the present economic and political situation, both national and international, support and direction on the part of the state are inevitable. In other words, economic liberalism of the strict type no longer exists, because it is no longer possible.

Economically, in the biggest democratic country, the United States of America, it has not yet been decided whether, at least for the immediate future, the government is to control industry and its big cartels, or the big cartels the government, or whether the trade unions will be powerful enough to exercise their influence on both. It is not impossible that out of the pending situation new multiple forms of business and production will emerge, something similar to the Swedish "middle way," or a system of economic, cultural, and political councils in which experienced men and women can co-operate with the government in the great endeavor to strike the balance between control and freedom. But it is just as possible that in the end neither the democratic state nor the cartels nor the trade unions, but some forms of collectivism of the fascist or communist type will issue from the present struggle of powers. This issue will not be decided by economics or politics alone, but by the practical answer to the question as to what degree the precious heritage of true liberalism, namely the ideas of toleration and of the "natural" or "inalienable" rights of man are still a living factor in our present society. If they are not, then the falling structure of economic liberalism will inevitably take with it the genuine elements of freedom, and we will enter into a new era of force and control.

Nothing could be so conducive to this failure of the democratic principle as the attitude of fear which in these days seems to obsess the economically more privileged groups of all countries. Truly, there is necessity for decent conservatism in any political situation; the advancing forces need checking and criticism as much as the retarding. But modern conservatism is without ideas, without constructive principles, without courage, and thus does everything to destroy itself. Its followers supported Hitler, inside and outside Germany, because they saw in him an instrument to quench the menace of communism; in France before 1940 they disintegrated the defensive powers in their own country because they disliked its government; in England they decided to go to Munich; in the United States they ousted Willkie and presented Dewey; and, after years of war, international derangement, and talks about peace they are without any clear policy with regard to the future organization of the world. Democratic muddle stands against communist purposefulness.

The reason for this decay of conservatism is that it blinds itself against the inherent necessities of our time and thus puts itself out of gear with the most pressing forces in our present historical situation, leaving to its most radical opponents the privilege of exercising increasing influence over the minds of the masses. In his state of constant anxiety the typical modern conservative is afraid even of any scientific approach to political problems; he helps in the ousting of liberal professors, in preventing students from the discussion of their most urgent problems under competent guidance, thus exposing them to unguided chance decisions; he refuses to pay taxes—but pays willingly for propaganda agencies which prosper from the stupidity of his fear. With regard to the enlightenment of mankind he behaves similarly to the Catholic and Protestant hierarchy which in the centuries after the Renaissance lost its influence on educated men because of its fear and censorship of everything which meant progress. In theological circles—in some at least—one begins to see both the failure and the lack of necessity in such an attitude. Will our conservative groups understand it before it is too late, as it has already become too late on the whole European continent?

But let us now return to our historical analysis of the role of liberalism, and especially of its relation to the state.

The following effects have resulted from the fact that in the era of liberalism the people and the state became increasingly interdependent.

The character of wars has changed. We no longer have wars of dynasties because it is no longer an issue whether the House of Hapsburg, or the House of Bourbon, or the House of Hohenzollern wishes a piece of land claimed by another prince. Instead the power impulse, which so far has been inherent in every great political organization, expresses itself now in more extended groups of the population. In European countries the hereditary nobility allied itself first with the rich industrial and financial upstarts thus forming one of the most dangerous pressure groups in history. When this somewhat exclusive alliance lost in influence and public prestige it did not hesitate to use, under the disguise of patriotism, the forces of despair and criminality emerging in some countries as a consequence of political and economic distress. In this way it perpetuated and even strengthened its influence for a while. But it failed to envisage that the new auxiliary troops of fascism would soon claim the role of the master, overthrow the conservative-liberal order through identifying themselves with the state, and accelerate the plunge of the whole world into chaos.

It added to the defeat of the older, more aristocratic liberalism that the modern wars need not only gigantic armies, but also mass production with similarly enormous armies of workers. This has given to modern wars a character of totalitarianism and a degree of horror and destruction in comparison to which the older dynastic wars with their small armies of professional soldiers were a relatively petty affair. Only those earlier wars in which general religious fanaticism could be harnessed to the chariots of dynastic ambitions, as for example the Thirty Years' War, can compare in violence with our modern total warfare.

As an inevitable concomitant to the decay of the liberal society there arose the oppositional ideology of socialism. First despised and laughed at, like the early Christian church, it gathered momentum with every new social catastrophe. Under its banner assembled not only the working classes of Europe, but also uprooted and socially conscientious intellectuals. Thus a powerful trend toward collectivism grew from different sides into the supposedly strong fiber of the capitalist society. We are now at that juncture of history when the dynamic of the stream of collectivism has broken through the surface and demands decision.

This challenge will not be met by the defeat of fascism, which was nothing but a temporary outgrowth of the social confusion described in the previous paragraphs. Nor will the shattered building of Western society be restored by occasional repairing of this or that crack in its walls. Rather we need a fundamental and unprejudiced re-thinking of our social problems and a power of synthesis such as history for hundreds of years has not demanded from men. In the practical world of affairs, especially in business and politics, we need a combination of co-ordination and initiative, and in the world of the Spirit we need a new body of firm convictions in which, however, liberty is respected as one of the constituent elements. For despite all failures of capitalist liberalism, the claim of genuine liberalism will remain an eternal concern of man under any economic and political structure. This claim is to have a society of men working together with the hope for progress under a just state and in a climate of dignity and freedom.

But welfare and freedom within each single nation cannot be achieved without a larger commonwealth of nations which should restore the faith of man in a certain stability of human relations. He must not be exposed to the continual fear that the effect of the work of his hands and his mind is annihilated by the clash of gigantic powers which he cannot control; in addition he must regain some faith that he and his nation are participating in a total endeavor of humanity to overcome the demons of war and destruction in a common, though hard, struggle for progress and civilization. Without such an embracing faith the individual struggle of man loses much of its meaning. It becomes a matter of survival and competition, instead of a great and inspiring enterprise.

Even though, under the impact of the present suffering, the intellectual effort of man has slackened into fatigue and reaction, this cannot last for generations. The rational spirit which we connected with the culture of ancient Hellas and which re-emerged in Western civilization in the times of the Renaissance, cannot stay long in a convent of resignation. Whatever the faults of the modern mind may be, at least it is experimental. It has been trained to observe and to search for truth in a process of trial and error. Consequently it resists long repose, authority, and deprivation of freedom. It sees history more in evolutionary and developmental than in static forms.

Thus, whether we like it or not, we cannot return to the past and rest peacefully in its shadow. If we tried, we would have neither peace nor rest but only decay. Without illusions about the difficulty of the task ahead we must attempt to forge our spiritual conflicts into a new synthesis in which are united search and faith, realism and transcendentalism, respect for the great in the tradition, and belief in progress. Only with such convictions about the meaning of man can we find means to apply the gigantic growth of science and industry for constructive purposes, instead of allowing them to develop their own momentum without regard for humanity.

So far as the particular problem of the state and of industry are concerned we have to distinguish clearly between the essential qualities in the liberal tradition and the transient political or economic features of individualism. Without such clear separation of the unchangeable and the changeable facets in the structure of our civilization we are destined for confusion which will end in some kind of collectivism, whether it is of the kind we now call fascism or bolshevism.

Many do not even see the bottom of the conflict. They always think of merely political and economic tensions between the so-called democratic-capitalist and the totalitarian-communist conceptions of society. It is true that on the surface this appears to be the fundamental social conflict of the day. But the deeper conflict in which our period is involved is the confusion which both the capitalist and the communist societies have not yet been able to solve. It can be phrased in the following terms: Will men become only commodities in the hands of economic and political powers? Are we going to continue sending youth into wars, moving peaceful people around like cattle because they happened to be born within changing political boundaries, and depriving so-called backward nations of their freedom of political action? Or are we going to recognize practically what we are always talking about, namely the dignity of man as a rational, moral, and working being? Under the impact of these questions the great assignment of history to the Western nations after this war will be to avoid the fallacy of confusing one or the other form of external political and economic organization with concepts of right or wrong, democratic or undemocratic, dignified or undignified. Rather they must strive for an order which provides the basic social and psychological conditions as we have discussed them in the first two chapters of this book. If we are constantly afraid that we might lose democracy with every new reform which is necessary for the prevention of rising social evils, we will not scare away the dangers to democracy but democracy itself.

But man cannot acquire such an unprejudiced attitude of reason and courage when left to his own nature. Hence, the more people become desirous of a rational society the more they must also understand the necessity of cultivating systematically the constructive capacities of the human mind, in other words, the necessity of education.

Only such a faith can save us from the defeatist attitude which may easily overcome us when we view objectively all the unsolved dilemmas of the past and the present.

CHAPTER IV

EDUCATION

I. The Function of Education

IN HIS INTRODUCTION to a history of philosophy one modern scholar states that in works preceding his own he found more than ninety different definitions of philosophy. Therefore, instead of continuing such futile attempts, he decided to let philosophy itself appear in the whole richness of its meanings and endeavors, without forcing it into a strait jacket of definitions.

Education is similar. Any rigid determination of its properties and purposes would be futile. The only goal we can set ourselves in an attempt at defining the role of education within civilization is an understanding of the functions and aims which it will assume according to the prevailing needs and aspirations of different periods.

Insight into the dynamic and changing character of education has led some modern philosophers toward complete relativism not only with respect to its ways and means, but also with respect to its aims. According to them, our humble task is to understand why one period developed this, and another period another educational pattern, and then to use the knowledge thus gained for a more effective solution of the problems of our own period.

This relativist position, however laudable from the point of view of scholarly honesty, is nevertheless fallacious in two respects.

First, it forgets that historical life is not merely like a game of chess in which the men are moved from one of the sixty-four squares to another according to plans of powers they cannot imagine. Rather is history the result of a highly complicated mixture of forces. To be sure, men and nations are bound to certain physical and geographical conditions, and they cannot totally alter the effect of past and contemporary events on their present and future. In this respect all human life bears the character of relativity and contingency. On the other hand, history is made by human beings who are allowed to think, to decide, and to act. Thus those who describe the life of men and nations as a mere play of interrelationships or superior forces, give their fellow men a wrong picture. They will teach them to miss history, rather than to make it.

Secondly, it is only on the surface that history seems to develop constantly changing patterns. When our eyes reach through the ripple into the depth of history, we discover that its progress depends on the working of the social, spiritual, and psychological conditions as we described them in the previous chapters of this book. Of course, the realization of these conditions requires ever new acts and decisions according to varying environments. They are not given to man like rain and sunshine. They must be understood and created anew every day; they are fundamental requisites as well as results of effort.

In the process of understanding and realizing these perpetual conditions of civilization education is of decisive importance. It is one of the main instruments that enable civilized societies to survive and work, to reason and believe, to develop standards of excellence and the great sentiment of love, and finally, to understand the psychological conditions of individual existence. It is a life-long process, related to human life in the individual and social, as well as in the physical and mental aspects. Conceived of in this way, education receives a meaning completely different from narrow pedagogical concepts.

However, the customary connection of education with schools and teachers is not unjustified. For in schools, still more than in families, a systematic effort is made to impart the elements of knowledge into the minds of the young. And though knowledge is only a part of civilization, it is nevertheless an important one, requiring systematic thinking and skill on the part of the conveyor. In addition, the school aims not only at transmitting knowledge; it trains its students increasingly in vocational techniques. Furthermore, all great educators had in mind visions of a mature and rounded out personality. Finally, all modern nations understand that their cultural and political survival depends on an effective school system, for it is the most effective medium to transmit the standards and aspirations of a society from one generation to the other.

II. Levels of Education

If now we try to evaluate the role of the different levels of schooling within modern civilization, we find that the school level about which there is the least amount of controversy is the elementary school. This is the case not because it is fully satisfactory with respect to teaching, treatment of children, and housing—even in so-called advanced countries we can find scandalous conditions—but because the elementary school possesses relatively clear ideas about its objectives. It has to give its pupils that minimum of knowledge in the fundamentals of learning and that minimum of orientation about their natural and social environment which enable them to survive and to understand the elementary processes in the social organism. In addition, differentiation of talent, that great problem of education, does not yet imperil the unity of the elementary school structure to such an extent as it does on the higher levels. For the knowledge required in the elementary school is still of such a kind that the majority of normally gifted children are able to acquire it, though some with considerable difficulty.

This happy state ends with adolescence which, in most modern countries, marks at the same time the end of public elementary training. Differences in intellectual endowment and in social background begin to assert themselves. A society of children, if unexposed to disruptive influences from adults, is a relatively unified society. Ethnic background, the position of parents, and differences of talent do not play a great part. With adolescence not only the sexual, but also the social and intellectual problems begin. Therefore the modern secondary school offers almost insurmountable difficulties. Our ancestors had no idea of them because they reserved this school only for an intellectually and socially favored group, generally not for more than one to three per cent of young people between twelve and eighteen years of age. The difficulties emerged with necessity when more and more people demanded their share in advanced theoretical training not knowing that the favor they asked for was not always a pure blessing. For about forty per cent of young people are not so constituted as to really profit from abstract intellectual work the moment it goes beyond the tenth grade of a normal modern school system. They can become useful citizens and develop a certain degree of creativeness and inventiveness in practical life, but they cannot find their center of gravity in advanced intellectual endeavor; rather than profiting from it, they become frustrated by a primarily bookish type of learning.

The unity of the education of adolescents is disturbed also by their different vocational interests. This problem too did not exist up to about fifty years ago, when the majority of the young entered into practical work right after elementary school. Those who prepared for an academic profession were submitted to an obligatory liberal training. The purposes of this training were the formation of all-round educated personalities capable of incorporating specialized work into a broader framework of interests, the continuation of the genteel tradition, and the acquisition of the mental techniques, required for systematic thinking.

Liberal education then, in spite of its traditional emphasis on classical languages, was not intended to be "remote" or a preparation for life in an "ivory tower." For its great advocates, Erasmus of Rotterdam, Montaigne, and Wilhelm von Humboldt the liberal tradition was the best medium for the formation of an harmonious, rich, and imaginative personality. In addition, it was always interwoven with concrete interests of the professions which in earlier times demanded distinction not only in specialized knowledge, but also in cultural experience. It is, after all, with education as with the persons to whom it is applied: neither can flourish in a vacuum; both need a concretely felt purpose.

Thus, whenever a school system and its curriculum approximate a state of esoteric aloofness, they degenerate rapidly into Alexandrianism, estheticism, and snobbishness. On the other hand, there must exist in every advanced civilization an education which tells youth that they are born not only for a vocation, but also for becoming cultured human beings, and in advanced forms of such schooling a certain esoteric distance from the multitude is, unfortunately, inevitable. Hence, the criterion of the quality of a liberal education lies not necessarily in the recognition of its value by "everybody" who have perhaps never been capable of experiencing what it is. If the measure of "everybody" became general—as it threatens—then our whole civilization, our art, and our philosophy would sink down to the level of the popular magazine and the typical radio program, and even they would become increasingly vulgar for lack of criticism and incentive.

Rather the criterion of a liberal education lies in the degree to which its receivers are able and willing to use their superior training as a stimulus for courageous and creative thinking and doing, irrespective of whether, in this way, they acquire popularity or not. Or we could also say: If it is the aim of education generally, to acquaint man with the conditions of his civilization and his personal existence, it is the privilege and duty of advanced forms of liberal education to raise this knowledge up to a higher level of critical awareness and responsibility. If, therefore, the professional people

degenerate into a crowd of mere specialists, because specialization is the easiest and quickest way to success, and if the
secondary schools and universities, out of profit motives,
ignorance, and timidity, foster this development, not only
specialized research itself will deteriorate for lack of imagination, but civilization as a whole will be in jeopardy.

But in education just as much as in other fields of life we
suffer from the fatal tendency of the human intellect to erect
false conceptual barriers between essentially interconnected
values. Why should a liberal education be contrary to a useful education; why should theoretical knowledge be opposed
to applied knowledge; and why should abstract and concrete
thinking exclude each other? These activities are co-operating in all productivity, in all mature persons and mature societies; therefore they must also be interrelated in education.

Of course, the degree of accentuation must change according to a person's ability and calling. Those who will enter
the workshop of practical life at a relatively early age ought
to be more quickly acquainted with the reality which they
will meet and which they can understand, whereas men in
the professions need richness of imagination and association,
the ability to compare and criticize, and last but not least, the
power to distinguish between the abiding and the transient in
the complicated web of values and opinions.

But before we will be able to solve the dilemma of modern education which lies in its double responsibility toward
the whole of civilization and specialized practical life, a number of conflicts will have to be reconciled. These conflicts
were an inevitable consequence of the rapid development of
modern society from a patriarchal and agricultural into a
modern democratic and industrial society; but now they must
be solved lest we get stuck midway and then gradually slide
back.

III. The Three Main Problems

There are three great sectors of education in which the hardest spade work will have to be done before we can reap a

good harvest. First we need more knowledge about the psychic conditions of childhood, second we need clearer ideas about the tasks and character of the modern curriculum, and finally a clearer policy in educational organization.

A. *The Psychological Problem*

Although great advance has been made in different fields of psychology, education still suffers from our insufficient knowledge of the inner problems of childhood and youth. This lack is all the worse since we cannot have a science of learning without an underlying and reliable science of the psychic development of the young.

To ask only one question, of what nature are a child's interests? Or, in other words, what is the psychic environment in which he lives, without being able to rationalize it and to explain it to adults? Certainly it is wrong to say, as we often do, that a child is interested merely in concrete things. Mostly he shows a strange ambiguity of interests. Like primitive peoples he is attracted by tangible things, but he also likes to dream; he loves the mystical and the fairy tale. Thus his mental environment is both the near as well as the distant and the fanciful.

This ambiguity is likely to last until late adolescence, and in many and perhaps the most gifted persons it lasts during their whole life. The artist and the creative thinker are probably those who have saved the best qualities of childhood through all maturation and sophistication. Therefore so many of them do not fit into the so-called "world of reality." Naturally, the young person's specific relation to the concrete and conceptual world modify his relation to everything he encounters and tries to understand. And as the adult lives in a different conceptual network he is most liable to misunderstand the child. Science will help little in this dilemma; love and intuition achieve much. Therefore the disappointing quality of books on child psychology, and the great wisdom of a loving mother with a healthy view of life.

Yet, in spite of the veil which hides from the adult even his own youth, certain characteristics seem to be evident. During childhood the urges and emotions dominate more than during adulthood. Elements of rationality are not absent, just as—reversely—we find in the soul of the adult a large element of irrationality. But in the life of a child rational thinking has not yet assumed the role which we expect it to play in a mature person. Order in a child's life is determined more from outside than from within. Hence it is one of the tasks of education to help the young in finding an organic transition from a primarily emotional into a somewhat rational ego. This transition is one of the most difficult processes in life; only few persons go through it without some scars, and many never succeed at all.

One of the usually suggested ways toward the formation of a socially useful and rational ego is habituation, or as modern psychology likes to say, "conditioning."

There is much truth in the theory of conditioning, provided it does not arrogate the right to explain the totality of man's relation to himself, his fellow man, and the universe. But certainly our mores, taboos, judgments and prejudices are partly due to such conditioning. Plato, who in his *Republic* wished to set up the image of a completely stable society, was the first strong advocate of the theory of habit-forming.

But it is, in a way, significant that this theory appears exactly in Plato's *Republic*. For this work, in spite of all its profoundness, is in many respects "totalitarian"; its author considers freedom to be a privilege of only a few; he recommends censorship and a rather immobile society. And there also can be no doubt that the doctrinaire American theory of conditioning, namely behaviorism, must envisage human society much more as a beehive than as a democracy if it wants to stick to its original premises. But human life is human for the very reason that in it superior motives always interact with natural conditions. Certainly, the child learns that right habits are rewarded, and acts under the influence of this experience. He also acquires such feelings as love and gratitude originally in a very material relation between him and the mother who feeds and protects him. But in the course of time these merely "natural" relationships become selective principles for action and decision. The normally growing person wishes not only to receive benefits, he wishes to extend them to others, and thus accepts them as criteria for his own conduct.

The transformation of egotistic into altruistic motives, is the very essence of growth in sound ethical behavior. But the full satisfaction of the child's sound natural instincts is as necessary as the organic transfer from the ego to the alter ego. Without the first, morality does not moor in the deeper grounds of the personality and becomes a bundle of abstract "ideals," which either are deserted in critical moments or enter into an attitude of stiff self-righteousness, which also betrays a person's weakness. Without the second, the organic transfer, a person never transcends his Self. He will always try to be his own goal, and thus fail to find lasting and embracing purposes on which to live.

For all these reasons the first years of life are of utmost importance. They form the first and central circle of contact with things human and natural and help the human being to settle his growing self in the world. If these years are disturbed and unhappy, a person is likely to grow like a bush whose roots are too loosely connected with the nourishing substance of the soil.

The first years of life are so significant also because they represent the greatest accomplishment which the human being is capable of achieving in a relatively brief span of time. One could venture to say that the years between six and sixty are, speaking qualitatively, less rich in fundamental experiences than the years of early childhood. Therefore infancy is the most delicate age, both physically and mentally. And it is mostly due to later romanticizing, not corresponding to reality, that we like to describe the age of childhood and adolescence as one of mere bliss and joyfulness. Minor though the problems of the young seem to the adult, they can cut as deep furrows into the acre of the soul as the deepest sorrows of an adult.

In the last analysis, no child will ever be saved merely by the psychological knowledge of his parents or teachers. The main condition of educational success is that the child feel sheltered in an atmosphere of love in which he is understood without much talking. Even in such an atmosphere there may occur some misunderstanding, and punishment may be necessary. But even so the child does not feel himself in a state of loneliness in the face of a gigantic and threatening universe. Because as a child he had gone himself through such experiences, Friedrich Froebel, the father of the Kindergarten, wrote his famous words: "Come, let us live for our children."

B. *The Curriculum*

As we have seen, the first layer of experiences is already formed when, in about the sixth year of his life, the child is subjected to formal training in an elementary school. But this fact does not diminish the responsibility of this institution. For a careless form of elementary schooling with false relations of a child to his teachers and his comrades may still unsettle a young person and throw him and his family into tragic difficulties.

From the particular task of the elementary school, namely to continue the child's process of mooring in life and society, follows its particular curriculum. It cannot be primarily intellectual during the first four years. Whatever is being learned during this time must be learned as part of the training for the fundamental requisites of life, which are health, harmony between mind and body, sound emotions and loyalties, and a grasp of the most significant techniques of living in a modern society, such as reading, writing, and arithmetic. Consequently, not before the upper grades of the elementary schools should there begin a distinct division of learning into separate subjects. Even then the specific knowledge conveyed ought to be subservient to the endeavor of incorporating the young into the community, rather than making little experts in one or the other field.

The specialization and diversification of subjects characterize the beginning of non-elementary or secondary training. With it begins the difficulty of constructing a curriculum which does justice to the tripartite task of the secondary school: to develop a child's character and personality, to lay the foundation of knowledge which he needs in his later vocational and civil life, and to do justice to the diversity of talent as it appears more and more distinctly in the period of adolescence.

The term "curriculum" means originally a race track. If one transfers this analogy to many of our modern school programs, then there is certainly much running, but no goal to direct all the effort. This disquieting situation results from the understandable endeavor of the modern secondary schools to satisfy all the many claims of modern life on education, even though they cannot possibly be harmonized within one and the same framework.

The disintegration of the curriculum has been fostered by a kind of modern psychology which was not sufficiently aware of the purposeful design in personal growth and learning. Thus in the United States the quantitative system of separate courses with their "credits" and "points" could replace the traditional concept of a curriculum in which the different subjects were related to each other like chapters in a well-organized book. In this credit system, which is uniquely American, every item of learning is supposed to have more or less the same value as the other. So one can see records of American high school graduates in which a bit of language study, entirely insufficient to give the student an insight into a foreign language, stands beside some commercial English, some manual courses, and some natural sciences which are unsupported by any mathematical preparation. In the guidance or choices of the student often no other principle seems to have prevailed but that of least difficulty. Such a system is dangerous from the psychological point of view because it does not allow for steadiness and coherence in development and effort, and changes the process of education into a kind of hurdle race with innumerable tests and quizzes and other memory devices in the way of the runner; it is also detrimental to civilization because it represents to young people the cultural heritage more as a sum of skills than as the result of concerted cultural effort.

But if there exists no comprehensive philosophy of the curriculum which helps the teacher see what to put first and what to put last, the chance is that in the fight for a place in the program those subjects suffer most which the average teacher or school board member considers "remote" or "too difficult," regardless of whether or not they represent important parts of the body of civilization.

A curriculum, however, is not like a pile of stones which can be tossed around arbitrarily. One should better envisage it in form of a triangle in which one of the angles symbolizes the psycho-physical conditions of the child, his interests and talents; the second angle represents the knowledge and skills necessary for a society to produce goods, to survive, and to compete with other societies; and the third angle the ideals, aims, and values of human civilization. In loose analogy to Hegel's famous dialectical scheme one could also say that the first angle represents the subjective and personal, the second angle the objective and social, and the third angle the absolute and spiritual elements in life. The moment one changes or cuts off from the whole one of the three angles, the whole figure and its equilibrium become distorted.

One can prove this easily with reference to the history of education. In older times too much stress was laid on religion, and the specific needs of the child and of society were neglected. With the change of the cultural pattern from the Middle Ages toward the Renaissance a new ideal arose: the harmoniously and universally educated personality. Unfortunately, in too many cases this ideal degenerated into a primarily historical and encyclopedic form of instruction. In addition, the typical secondary and higher systems of education since the Renaissance have considered logical reasoning and knowledge the central agent in the development of civilization; thus little attention was given to individual differences and the cultivation of the emotional and active side of life. Religion, to be sure, remained part of the curriculum, but the majority of the teachers mistook historical knowledge about religion for an equivalent of true spiritual experience. Under the influence of these fallacies the older classical institutions, however excellent from the intellectual point of view, deceived themselves too easily about their real cultural value. Often they conveyed not culture in the sense of *cultura animi*, but knowledge which did not leave any recognizable traces in the mold of the personality.

In opposition to such one-sidedness the modern school has concentrated its attention on the child and his psychological conditions. Supported by modern psychology and humanitarian trends there developed, instead of the old subject-centered, the modern child-centered school. Here too, modern progressivism did not escape the danger of one-sidedness. It often failed to recognize the disciplinary and practical value of knowledge, and still more the necessity of connecting the inner life of the child to the superindividual values of humanity. Thus it often created a self-centered subjectivism without lasting purposes and loyalties, exposing the pupil in this way to even greater dangers than the somewhat routine-like older type of education.

However, in spite of mistakes in its experimental stage, progressive education has made teachers and parents aware of the specific conditions of childhood and learning. It has taught them that childhood is not a defect to be overcome as soon as possible, but a value in itself, a worthy object of study, a challenge and an obligation. In this respect progressive education has realized the dreams of the pioneers in education such as Comenius, Pestalozzi, and Froebel. With one grave limitation, however; it has not achieved the philosophical depth and wholeness out of which these men developed their educational ideas. And whenever a movement lacks in this quality, it is liable to lose the great perspective and to get stuck in techniques.

The lack of an embracing conception of education has also prevented us from finding a satisfactory solution of a problem already hinted at, namely of how to arrive at a synthesis between the principle of individualization and the necessity of unity within a national school system.

The more a young person matures and develops individual traits of personality, the more he is liable to refuse adverse, and to respond to adequate, motivations from outside. His life becomes a selective process. With respect to learning, the principle of individuality could be formulated as follows: only if the object to be learned fits the individual mental structure of the learner, can learning become a process of inner enrichment. Or, as Emerson, following Lao-tse, has said with his genius for brilliant formulation: "The only entrance so to know is so to be."

On the other hand, the recognition of individual differences in the learning process must not cause us to abandon the ideal of a common, or general, education. First because there is, despite all diversity, much communality of interest among the different types of men. And even if it did not exist to the degree it does, it would have to be insisted upon for the purpose of guaranteeing some unity of culture and communication among men. Therefore, even a high school or college with ideal differentiation should furnish for its students a unifying body of instruction in subjects of common human value.

To these subjects belong the rights and duties of a citizen, provided instruction in this field is not merely intellectual but connected with experience and action. Furthermore the dramatic, the musical, and the visual arts offer a wide range of common experience, as do sport, hygiene, and last but not least, manual work. Teachers ought to be more aware of the fact that the common element in the life of men lies not so much in their intellectual pursuits, as in their urges, abilities, and emotions. We are one by our hearts and hands; the intellect divides us. Therefore, general instruction must not force all students into an intellectual strait jacket, but must appeal to the more physical and emotional qualities and cultivate them through joined experiences. If schools, out of a misunderstood concept of equality, insist on intellectual uniformity they will all arrive at the same level of mediocrity, unsatisfactory to both the theoretically gifted student who receives too little, as well as the intellectually weak student for whom it is too much.

Even in advanced specialized training the ideal of a general education does not need be abandoned. It is one of the most tragic, though frequent, mistakes to think that specialization means necessarily narrow technicalization. Of course, generalization and specialization are mutually exclusive if general education is understood in primarily quantitative terms, that is so-and-so-much language, history, mathematics, and science for all students together, and if, on the other hand, all vocational and professional training is merely a teaching of tricks.

But is not all good education an endeavor to show the essential unity of man's search for truth in the very variety of its methods and contents? Under such auspices general education and right differentiation of specialization do not contradict, but supplement each other. For only through reference to its greater and general context does special training become meaningful and interesting, and only through specialization and application is the common heritage of culture and knowledge vitalized and extended.

Therefore the vocational teacher fails his educational purpose if he explains to his pupils the use of a lathe in merely mechanical terms without showing that it is an ingenious application of universal laws of nature.

Similarly the teacher who teaches medieval history primarily as a succession of so-and-so-many popes, kings, and wars represents the illiberal and banausic type, proud though he may be of his humanities. But he is truly general and liberal if he explains the Middle Ages as a phase of the gradual reconstruction of European culture through faith in universal human ideals, if he makes understandable the conflict between the principles of the *ecclesia militans* and the secular estates, and if he demonstrates to his students the necessity of strong convictions for the maintenance of tradition and the dangers inherent in all dogmatism and in the adoration of institutions as ends in themselves. Finally, in connection with the Middle Ages, he can illustrate the eternal human tragedy which always emerges when the representatives of ideas in their fight with early powers use the instruments of the enemy and thus become relativistic, imperialistic, and hypocritical.

The uninspiring teacher of the humanities can do even more harm than a mediocre vocational teacher, for the latter conveys to his students at least some practical knowledge, whereas from the poor teaching of the humanities nothing remains but a feeling of boredom, instead of a sense of reverence for the great achievements and conflicts of mankind.

The salvation from the superficiality of modern civilization cannot come if the representatives of the "liberal arts," who are often incredibly ignorant of the realities of life, look down at the "technicians" and try to defend their weakening position by enforcing some unrelated courses in the humanities on the prospective scientist and engineer whose workday is already overcrowded. The salvation can come only through generalization or humanization in and of whatever field. This, of course, needs common, comparative, and general knowledge. Unfortunately, such knowledge is rare. But without it education can never represent the noblest aspirations of society and remind men of their being part of humanity, not only as it is, but as it ought to be.

C. *Organization: The School of the Future*

The bewildering situation of modern education is reflected in its external structure. We live in an age of continual change of school systems and school types. And as the cur-

riculum of the secondary school is most intensely in a stage
of transformation, so also is its organization.

The older European "bifurcated" system, which had one
big track through the elementary and vocational schools, and
a very narrow track for the one to three per cent of the
population who prepared for an academic profession, no
longer works, simple though rather unjust as it was. The
first country to break away from it was the United States
with its "academies" and its public high schools, and now we
distinguish generally between the European bifurcated and
the American single-track system. No doubt the American
system is more democratic, and, for this reason, has been the
object of attention of liberal-minded educators in the European countries, especially after 1918. Yet, the older European structure has stood its ground, though it underwent
democratic modifications in the era between the two World
Wars.

Was this perseverance due only to the desire of the conservative classes to preserve their privileged position? Certainly the highly selective type of the classical preparatory
school was, in a way, linked up with the old European
feudal and plutocratic structure, though at least on the continent, not at all to the degree which American educators
assume. But besides conscious or unconscious egotistic tendencies there was a serious question whether the wholesale introduction of the American single-track system might lead
to a decrease in the intellectual quality of secondary schooling. A graduate of a good continental secondary school had,
in the better times of Europe, a good taste for his vernacular
and its literature, he possessed a reading knowledge of three
to four foreign languages, he knew mathematics up to the
calculus, he was sufficiently acquainted with the natural sciences to have an idea of the experimental method and the
main laws of nature, and he had been taught sufficient history
to be aware of the main trends of European civilization,
though seen mainly in the light of the past and a specific
national ideology.

Compared with these achievements the American high school offers no great incentive for the scholarly mind. Of course, the rather large part of American citizens who have finished high school have a slightly better education and certainly a more outspoken democratic self-consciousness than the socially comparable European citizen with only elementary and vocational education. Many of the graduates from the older classical schools of Europe were bookish, snobbish, and often spoiled for practical pursuits of life, whereas American boys and girls are unspoiled by too much literacy, more open minded, and more humane. On the other hand, the rigid secondary schools of old Europe produced an intellectual *élite* which up to the nineteenth century created an international community of educated men who understood each other in spite of national rivalry; they produced remarkable results in scholarship and enabled even countries with small physical resources to compete culturally with the bigger or richer nations. Unless great revolutionary upheavals throw the whole social and intellectual tradition of Europe overboard—which is not unlikely—the European nations probably will not abandon their selective school system, even after this present war. Rather it looks as if the glowing optimism of the American educators concerning the single-track system were already undergoing modifications.

There occur more and more divisions and subdivisions in the upper grades of the elementary school and the high schools; trade and technical schools develop in increasing numbers besides the common track; the junior college with its emphasis on more practical subjects and semi-professional training invades the so-far sacred sphere of the liberal arts college; and in preparation for graduate schools students tend to devote more and more time to pre-professional, rather than to general studies. All tends toward the acceptance of a more articulated system even on the democratic American continent. For this articulation conforms with the psychological principle of differentiation and appar-

ently satisfies the needs of industry and the professions better than a mechanical single-track system.

On the other hand, there is in the United States this precious heritage of a common democratic education, and there
is a Europe torn by class hatred and international wars, with
whole countries menaced by the peril of barbarism. What,
after all—one may ask—has all this highly selective education produced?

Which way then will America have to choose for the
education of its own youth?

The answer is: unite where unity is possible and differen-
tiate where differentiation is requisite for growth and productivity. If we ask for a guiding principle in this combined
policy of unification and articulation we have to refer to our
discussion of the curriculum. There we stated that the communality of men is in their urges and emotions, whereas the
distinction comes up in their intellectual pursuits.

Consequently the ideal American high school of the future
would be a complex of buildings, workshops, fields, stables,
and gardens with large premises. In one building all pupils
would assemble for the common cultivation of their emotional life through worship, music, and dramatic perform-
ances. In this building also the great masterpieces of the
visual arts would be exhibited. Another building would contain the workshops and studios in which all students would
learn some craft and try their talent in one of the creative
arts. Almost every normal person can find some channel for
satisfactory esthetic self-expression. A third building would
be for play and sport. These three houses would be the
uniting center of the school; also the common meals would
be served in one of them.

Around these central buildings which belong to all would
be those for the more specialized purposes as they arise from
the necessity of differentiation and articulation. One building would harbor the young humanists mainly interested in
historical, linguistic, literary, and philosophical studies. The

second building would be the house for the young scientists, with a museum of natural history and laboratories; the third for the future young administrators and businessmen, and the fourth for the young artisans.

Each of these buildings, in spite of its dedication to a specific group of pupils, should also serve the common purpose of the whole school as much as possible. For the cultivation of the historical interests of the pupils the house of the humanists could provide equipment and incentives; the young scientists could offer their help wherever a scientific problem arose which could be of interest to the total school; the young administrators and businessmen ought to be of assistance to the administrative staff and connect the school with the community, showing again that education is not an isolated affair, but a part of society. Finally the young manual workers would be those who, while learning their trade, would produce part of the technical apparatuses and other equipment for the school community. Together with the scientific department they would be the leaders of the others when repairing has to be done, and in this way learn that much of their work is but an application of the scientific principles which the more scientifically minded comrades explore in theoretical fashion.

In such a new school community those with limited powers of mind can learn at least some basic manual skills and can help in the gardens and the kitchens. Furthermore, they will be together with the other groups during the hours commonly dedicated to devotions, art, sport, and manual work. None, not even the most theoretical young highbrow, ought to be freed from these hours, nor from common practical work in the fields and stables. Many intellectuals are, in spite of their logical skill, kind of social misfits for the very reason that the totality of their nature has not been allowed sufficient incentive and development. In this way a society trains specialists but never leaders. Therefore in the future we must take seriously Pestalozzi's demand for simultaneous education of "the brain, the heart, and the hand." And today, when young people remain so much longer in school than in earlier times, we have to include into the orbit of education training in practical responsibility. We often expose young people, at an age when a hundred years ago they founded a farm in the Middle West or sailed the seas, to no other influence than that of school masters, school mistresses, and tutors. Thus we help to bring up people who spend their lives in waiting for assignments and help from above rather than in pioneering and democratic living. Combined with the general trend toward political centralization, such an education fits men marvelously for totalitarianism.

The school of the future, therefore, does not just play around with artificial forms of "self-administration," but gives its students a large opportunity to manage their own affairs. The leaders of the common activities in whatever field would be selected from the different departments equally; they would form one of the various bodies through which the pupils participate in the work and responsibilities of their little republic.

And why should such a school not become the natural community center which is so necessary for modern adult life and adult education? Why should it not offer its buildings and grounds for the community orchestra and the community theater, for adult education courses, and for the training of men and women in healthy living? Several schools in different countries which have tried to attract not only the children, but also the parents, have not only doubled but multiplied their influence on their communities.

The school of the future, as we have projected it, may appear to many as utopian. A utopia it is, but of no other kind than all the guiding ideas of mankind when they first were envisaged in the minds of a few. When Comenius in the terrific times of the Thirty Years' War asked for a universal and articulated public-school system with natural methods of teaching, he was a utopian. The early liberals, the early democrats, the early socialists—they all were utopians. It is perhaps the central defect of the modern teacher that he has become far too much his community's obedient servant, dominated by school boards and afraid of the frowning of a town Samurai. A good teacher has the right to consider himself the trustee of his community and even more, as the trustee of humanity. The most exorbitant demands of his profession with respect to a better training of youth would for a whole year cost less than a day of war. At the same time the investment demanded would be a part in the defense and development of the greatest treasure of a nation, namely the mental and physical health of its people.

IV. INTERNATIONAL EDUCATION

Only if we have schools which form the personality of the student in accordance with his individuality and ground him, at the same time, deeply in the cultural heritage and communality of his people, only if we teach self-reliance together with sympathy, and tolerance together with firm convictions about the nature of humanity, only then can we hope to train young people for the understanding of their international responsibilities.

It is a sign of modern amateurishness and pseudo-intellectualism to think that we make better world citizens if we add to the already overcrowded curriculum some instruction about South America, or Asia, or Russia. Surely, we ought to find out how much knowledge of international problems could be intertwined with a pupil's knowledge of himself, his nation, and the natural and divine universe. But unless the pupils have already planted themselves in a ground of well-mastered experiences and human relations, it makes no sense to acquaint them with scattered bits of knowledge about the past and present of distant countries. Such information produces only the smattering semi-knowledge which is characteristic of a type of modern people who are nowhere really at home and consquently without roots and direction for their thinking and acting.

The best and perhaps only way to learn something about

foreign peoples is to live with them, after one feels at home with himself and his own nation. Therefore, in addition to the grounding work to be done at home, it would be the best international education to invite teachers and students of foreign countries and ethnic groups to live for some time together, and especially within a school of the kind just pictured. Such community experience would break down regionalism, guard against chauvinism and, on the other hand, protect young people from utopian ideas about universal world harmony. Many a man has learned to love foreign peoples from partaking in their folk dances; but in order to know them he must also have talked with them about their political conflicts, hopes and hatreds, and about these one speaks only to friends.

For the provision of international contact through education individual institutions, especially the great universities, can do very much. And the more that governments and bureaucratic authorities can be kept in a state of benevolent nonintervention, the better it is. When they become too influential the danger is always great that education becomes an instrument of nationalism or "cultural propaganda" rather than the symbol of the universal conscience of humanity, anchored in a person's experience of sharing and responsibility within his own people.

The enormous task involved in the cultural reconstruction of the world will make necessary an international agency which works with the different national school systems, research institutes, and associations of scholars and artists as the representative of the common aspects and interests of mankind irrespective of all national differences.

Whatever the future of our international relations will be, whether the hopes for permanent peace among men will be realized in the long run or disappointed, in either case it will be possible to have an International Organization for Educational and Cultural Co-operation, as it was possible during the past decades of international chaos to have an International Labor Office. This International Office would be the place toward which teachers, pupils, and schools of all levels could turn in whatever endeavor to foster international contacts. It would be the place which provides exchange of students, teachers and scholars, which tries to influence the radio and movie for the benefit of mankind, which gives council to national governments willing to profit from the experiences of other countries, and which stands behind the international universities which will have to be founded in the future.

Innumerable would be the tasks of such an office, but none of them would be greater than that of providing a supernational center which could symbolize to all men the noblest duty of education, namely, not only to make good citizens out of men, but to make good men out of citizens.

However, every agency cannot but reflect the spirit inherent in the persons and activities which it represents. Thus the future International Organization for Education could easily degenerate into a mere booking agency and information bureau with hundreds of desks and dictaphones, or into an arena of diplomatic bargaining like the old League of Nations, unless education, scholarship, and the arts maintain their own dignity and mission, rather than becoming auxiliaries of national diplomacy.

Thus this discussion about international education eventuates into the same demand which was already raised with respect to education within individual nations. There must be a spirit of universality strong enough to represent a firm and independent force of conscience against all the splitting relativities and contingencies of power and government.

This is the decisive problem not only with respect to the future International Organization for Education, but with respect to the future of our total civilization. Either education, art, philosophy, and religion again feel their community in a spiritual dimension of existence deeper and more embracing than anything which relates merely to the fleeting fractions of life, or they all will be driven into serving forces which prepare the desiccation and decay of Western civilization.

But do we still possess a possibility for building up such a community of men in the realm of spirit? This question, though it was intrinsic in the whole discussion on education, nevertheless transcends these boundaries; it will be dealt with more fully in the following chapters on art, politics, and philosophy.

CHAPTER V

ART

"The sense of the beautiful is God's
best gift to the human soul."
—W. H. Hudson

THE ROLE OF ART in civilization cannot be sufficiently understood unless we distinguish between art as the creative act of the artist, and art as a pervasive element in the life of individuals and society.

I. CREATIVE ART

Why do some people feel an inner compulsion to express themselves through the medium of art? There is probably some physical reason. Their specific hereditary endowment and their whole physical structure is of such a kind that, under a conducive environment, their intense vitality develops a powerful urge toward esthetic self-relief. This vitality and its kind of expressiveness result from a particular quality of the glandular and hormonic system, from a highly developed spiritual and sensuous susceptibility, and from an interaction of all these functions of our organism which causes us to enjoy sounds, colors, harmony, proportions, and the beauty of ideas.

But more interesting than the physiological is for us the psychological background of creative art.

Also the average man may sometimes feel a strong formative urge. The talented amateur may occasionally produce a painting or a poem. But for the genuine artist Form is not

136

one of the many nice and casual adornments of life, rather it is the element on which he lives. The amateur can be happy without using esthetic form as a means of communication or, if he uses it, it is not of definite and cogent character. For him different esthetic forms are often interchangeable; he may think he could paint, or compose a melody, or write a poem, be it either in blank verse, or a sonnet or a terza rima. For the artist, on the contrary, Form is fate; he does not choose it, rather it chooses him. He feels himself more as the instrument of a power which works in him, than the agent of his own free will. He does not add Form to an otherwise formless world, but the world itself is for him abundant with Form. The moment the excitement of an immediate experience begins to organize itself within him, a vision of *Gestalt* flows through his soul, first perhaps vague and groping, but gradually ordering into firm and steady proportions.

The specific relation to Form marks not only the difference between the artist and the amateur, but also between the artist and the interpreter, whether he be the actor, virtuoso, or literary critic. The interpreter projects himself into a work of art often to the degree of absorption, but the work itself exists *for* him and not *through* him. He reproduces, but does not produce.

The form element in the creative artist would be impossible without another quality which distinguishes him from the majority of his fellow men; namely, an unusual depth of experience. The artist is always abnormal, for he is supernormal. But this supernormality may create grave inferiorities in fields of life where every business clerk and preacher feels comfortably at home.

Artistic production which lacks depth of experience is not art in the profound sense of the word. It is artistry. It is like sensuality without love, in other words, prostitution. And nobody becomes more irritated by artistry than the artist; like a priest whose sanctuary is invaded by unbelievers.

Of what kind is the experience of the artist, in addition to the form element which we have already found in it?

Let us first remove some popular mistakes.

The fact that a work of art issues from an unusual intensity of feeling does not warrant the notion that the artist represents merely the emotional type of men, or that art is, so to speak, nothing but the effluence of bursting mental agitation.

This opinion forgets several decisive factors in the genesis of a good work of art. Certainly, it cannot be created without passion. Therefore often the routine of a vocation or of married life kills the artist, or he breaks out of its conventions. But there were marriages with ever renewed unity and Eros, and they made still greater artists because they gave them inner peace and concentration. Though the artist cannot produce when the creative excitement is gone, not every passion leads toward art. Passion alone would never have sufficed to create Elizabeth Barrett Browning's *Sonnets from the Portuguese*. Behind such creations must be something more: some god such as Diotima describes to Socrates under the name of Eros, the son of poverty and of plenty, or of longing and of abundance. The passion of the artist has not only a merely personal and egotistic, but a cosmic quality; it must occur in a great soul, though perhaps a restless one. There is no art without character.

Nor does the emotionalist concept of art sufficiently respect the practical implications of the form element. During the process of creation it transforms itself into the sometimes crucial reality of hard, good workmanship. Certainly a painter sometimes sketches a vivid scene in a few minutes, or a composer or poet sometimes works as though under dictation of a foreign power. But any life of a great artist proves the necessity of enormous endurance in craftsmanship combined with ever renewed inspiration of ideas. We possess different versions of some of the most easily flowing poems of world literature; they show that their charm and convincing form are the result of long and hard endeavor. In the Rodin museum at Paris we see how the great sculptor made one trial after another before he was satisfied with the expression of despair in the faces and bodies of "The Burgesses of Calais." The mental energy involved in the creation of Dante's *Divine Comedy* is as great as that required for the *Summa Theologiae* of Thomas Aquinas.

The final stage in the genesis of a profound work of beauty is probably one into which a large element of intellectual activity has entered, in spite of all nonintellectual or superintellectual properties of art. To be sure, this kind of "intellectual activity" is not logical and discursive as that of the scholar, but neither is it unlogical, or alogical; it represents a special form of human insight. It is intuition and comprehensive vision, often combined with extremely subtle and detailed observation, introspection and empathy with other beings—be they humans, plants, or animals. There is also a large element of contemplation in many forms of art, contemplation understood as the practice of meditating upon the deeper meanings and relationships in the universe of man and nature. We could call all these qualities together "esthetic intelligence," in contrast to "scientific intelligence."

In a way, "esthetic intelligence" is the finest organ of mental apperception we possess. It reaches down into the dim twilight of mental reality and raises upon the level of awareness feelings and ideas which otherwise would remain in the opaque sphere of the subconscious. Through this continual historical process of turning outward the inward treasures and dangers of the human soul, the artist makes one of the greatest contributions to civilization. Aeschylus, Dante, Shakespeare, and Goethe; or Palestrina, Bach, and Beethoven; or the masters of the Parthenon and of Chartres; Michelangelo, and Rembrandt signify not only new steps in the development of their arts, or in hearing and seeing, not even only new steps in understanding human situations; rather they signify new strides in the evolution of the human race from relative gloominess of feeling toward new stages of psychic refinement. Thus art has become an essential element in human culture, like ethics, religion, and thought. No agent in civilization, to give only one concrete illustration, has helped to refine our erotic life so much as the great artists' interpretation of beauty, love, and womanhood. Not even morality and religion have done so; on the contrary, they often have contributed more to the degradation than to the elevation of Eros.

For all these reasons it is dangerous to civilization to consider art a mere instrument in the pursuit of pleasure and amusement. An activity which is accompanied by pleasure, exists therefore, not merely for pleasure's sake but may have much deeper causes and completely different goals and inspirations. Life, of which art is a reflection and an expression, is not only pleasure and non-pleasure.

If we want to define the character of art most comprehensively we have to say that it is the esthetic expression of symbolic truth. Through the power we called "esthetic intelligence," the artist reaches through the surface of reality into its deeper meaning, rhythm, and beauty. All real art is transparent for the artistically minded person, as are religious symbols for the religious, and mathematical symbols for the mathematician. The bad mathematician learns the formula by heart, but cannot derive it, the pseudo-religious believes in the vestment of the dogma without grasping its cosmic significance, and for the unartistic person art is a decoration rather than a revelation of life. But the good painter never produces a mere photograph of reality (though some photographers may succeed in stealing deep glimpses from the ever changing face of nature); the good sculptor never simply transmutes human bodies into stone and cast; the poet or artistic writer never "describes," and the work of the composer who has no other medium for symbolizing the forces of nature but to imitate the noise of storms and thunder certainly does not exhale the true spirit of music.

Great art is not without reality, as it is not without intellect, but it is not only these. It is always discovery, though not of the scientific kind; it is always experience, though not empiric. The scenes pictured in Dostoevski's novels were not actual, but they contain more true and profound psychology than all psychological textbooks together. Therefore Aristotle can state "that poetry is both more philosophic and more penetrating than history." And there are the Pythagorean and Augustinian conceptions of music as a reflection of the divine harmony in the universe. A modern scientist may call this idea fantastic. Yet, in intention the pagan and the Christian philosophers were correct. They show the same reverence for music which fourteen hundred years later Schopenhauer expresses in his *The World as Will and Idea:*

Supposing it were possible to give a perfectly accurate, complete explanation of music, extending even to particulars, that is to say, a detailed repetition in concepts of what it expresses, this would also be a sufficient repetition and explanation of the world in concepts, or at least entirely parallel to such an explanation, and thus it would be the true philosophy.[1]

A poem describing the reaction to Bach's music expresses the philosophical meaning of art in a more artistic fashion:—

This is the mystery never understood:
A human mind beholds Eternity,
And She descends and manifests to him
Her depth and laws and language, and commands
That he translate them to the human race.

The stars of Heaven wander each alone
And yet in all-embracing unity,
While generations lift their eyes through night,
Are filled with reverence, and sense The Whole.
So in the Heaven of Spirit sound and symbol
Emerge and send through endless generations
Their rays sublime, transcendent, far away,
Filled with God's breath, and yet of us a part.
They build the golden bridges which connect
The little lives that die with all the great
That speaks of Him and feeds the fugitive
Events of restless men with sacred meaning.

[1] Arthur Schopenhauer, *The World as Will and Idea* (Boston: G. R. Osgood and Co., 1883), p. 342.

In consequence of the profoundly affective quality of art, people have often speculated about its relationship to such other great forces in human life as religion, or ethics, or the whole large realm of erotic experience. The historian could easily show that in the course of philosophical thought all these various phenomena have not only been related to each other, but each of them has been declared to be the cause of the other.

All such theories are one-sided because they see the center and source of the great aspirations of man in only one sector of our existence, as if the spiritual ground of life could be divided into separate lots. Instead we should believe that one kind of intensive experience renders the human soul ready also for the appreciation of the other great achievements in our mental evolution. Whenever a great sentiment captures us, it is always embracing and pervading, it transcends itself and evokes the latent powers in the adjacent regions of the soul. Profound love, deep sorrow from which we can recover, loyalty to a great cause, all this makes an individual richer, not only in respect to the one specific event, but in a whole variety of relations or, as we like to say, as a total person. Certainly, different individualities respond to the problems of life in predominantly esthetic, religious, ethical, or intellectual form. But if Plato is right when, in his *Phaedros*, he says that the Divine is "beautiful, good, wise and all that in unity" then all profound experiences, whether expressed in one or the other language, are comparable to the apexes of different pyramids all built on a broad common base. On the personal level, it is this particular structuring which gives an individual his special touch or atmosphere. We like it so much in a friend or beloved person, without ever being able, nor even willing to explain it fully.

Naturally, nowhere can we discover the potential wealth of psychic life to such a degree as in the genius. For he reaches most widely and deeply into the stream of creative excitement; hence he also exposes himself to the whole gamut of human joy and suffering. He symbolizes not only the blessing and benediction of mankind, he also carries its burden, and he learns from all.

Therefore it is impossible to place any creative genius exclusively into one category of interest and talent. He always shows a variety of qualities as does even every richly endowed person to a degree. These qualities order themselves in such a fashion that the one which becomes dominant, does not suppress the others. On the contrary, the dominant interest seems not only to be supported by the less dominant but, as a sort of grateful recognition for the service rendered, it vitalizes them in turn.

For the sake of illustration, let us divide the great geniuses of mankind first into the thinkers, presenting the group with the intellect as the dominant trend, second into the artists with the esthetic sense as the central interest, third into the religious men with their specific sense for holiness, and fourth into the ethical heroes of mankind, for whom service and sacrifice means the fulfillment of life. Then we will see that exactly the greatest representatives of each of these groups display in addition, or better in unity with, their dominant trend and achievement, certain subdominant capacities which often are of such a high quality that they deserve a place of honor for themselves.

The very greatest philosophers were not only masters in their own proper field. Plato, for example, was at the same time a poet; and who can say, whether Thomas Aquinas was greater as a rational than as a religious genius, or whether the logical discipline in the work of Kant is more admirable than his ethical energy? The great artists display an amazing variety of combined talents. Especially the writers run the whole scale from mystical and philosophical to empirical and observational interest. The poet Friedrich Schiller wrote one of the, if not the, profoundest essay on art, the "Letters on Esthetic Education." Among the composers Johann Sebastian Bach developed the art of counterpoint to almost mathematical precision. There seems to exist an intimate affinity between musical and mathematical language. Most of the great artists are profoundly religious. From the times of Dante up to the times of Paul Claudel and Rainer Maria Rilke the deepest about religion has been said by means of poetry and music rather than by means of theology.

On the other hand, intense religiousness is always a consummation of many seemingly different interests. Calvin and Kierkegaard, and again Thomas Aquinas were endowed with an unusual logical power; St. Augustine was one of the great artistic writers. And no great moral hero was only moral. Abraham Lincoln might have become a great lawyer or scholar if destiny had not foreseen him for other purposes. Albert Schweitzer, the modern humanitarian, was the greatest scholarly and musical interpreter of Bach's music, and a philosophical writer of importance. But he left the organ and his books and has become a physician and social worker among the Negroes in Africa.

Thus also a biographical analysis proves the fallacy of the question as to the priority of any one of the great modes of human self-expression. At the bottom of experience they are united, as the different parts of the body are united in the very formation of the embryo. But it is the specific function of the creative artist to add to the different languages by means of which humanity expresses its profoundest experiences and verities the language of symbol and form.

Whenever a civilization no longer understands how to use and listen to this language it loses not only in color and joyfulness, but also in depth.

II. Art as a Pervasive Element

Just as an individual shows the amalgamation of a great variety of experiences and values, so civilization unites many varying elements. It does so to such a degree that we have difficulty in separating the contribution of one element from those of the others. In addition, in the ebb and flow of civilization the force of each wave works upon the shape and direction of all the other waves. But whereas, everybody is convinced of the influence of the intellect on the most diverse human pursuits, many are inclined to think that art is something separate; a luxury, as it were, which could just as well be dispensed with.

As a matter of fact, everything is, in one way or another, touched by art. It may well be that the mass fabricated furniture in our modern rooms is more offensive to the esthetic taste than that which in earlier times a peasant hewed out from the trees in his wood; nevertheless, behind almost every instrument of modern life is a designer, educated or mis-educated in an art school. At present, art of some fashion surrounds us more than religion, and perhaps even more than reason. At least, many people like to be animated by some kind of art who do not bother about religion and who reason very little or not at all.

However, this visible influence of art on our external life is but a part of the story. There is something more penetrating about it, namely its subtle effect on the mold of personality.

Two men take a walk through nature. The one sees the beauty of the colors and lines around him, and the workshop of nature reveals to him the secret of a master hand. He is not a creative artist, but he has senses which, without his knowing, may have been trained by esthetic experience of some kind.

Another man, in minutes of happy leisure, has his mind floating on the melody of a waltz by Chopin, and if he is in grief he resorts to one of the great pieces of choral music. He would not be able to compose any of these melodies, but he lives in a world miles above the vulgarity or sentimentality of our so-called popular music. There is melody in his life; in all likelihood he has also good paintings or reproductions on his walls, and is selective in friendship. He can do so because people like the stimulation of his company.

There is a teacher who has flowers in his classroom and has trained the children to take care of them. From time to time he mixes a poem into his instruction, and whenever there is an opportunity to relate a subject to a work of art, he does so. The children prefer him and his teaching to that of other teachers though they do not know exactly why. Perhaps they feel that he understands them better than even the school psychologist with his tests and questionnaires. The parents tell each other that after some months of this teacher's influence the children are more polite at home and take up the reading of good books. Also this teacher may not be "creative," may not have acquired a Ph.D., nor contributed any articles to a journal. But his principal knows that his loss would change the value of the school.

Can civilization thrive without people like these? It certainly cannot. They are the many rootlets which connect the tree of civilization with the nourishing soil of inspiration.

The blessings which all mankind receives from art involve a similarly great responsibility on the part of the public, first in respect to the creative artist himself, second in respect to the things of art which surround us, and third in respect to the people who in daily life are able to enjoy the benefits of esthetic experience.

Concerning the creative artist himself, it has often been said that genius is a gift of the Lord; it cannot be bred artificially. Certainly not. But potential genius can be prevented from growing. There have been periods in every great European nation when destiny was particularly magnanimous in the generation of great men. In Italy it was the period of the Renaissance from Dante up to Michelangelo, in England that of Marlowe and Shakespeare, in Spain that of Cervantes and Lope de Vega, in France that of Corneille and Racine, in Germany that of Leibnitz and Bach up to Goethe. Each of these "classical" periods came about after a long and slow ripening of culture; they were, in addition, times of heightened national self-consciousness combined with expansion of international horizon. All rich productivity, in nations as well as in individuals, issues from a combination of growth in self-awareness and of absorption of new elements of thought.

Other factors also seem to have been conducive to the creation of genius; for example, a certain amount of stimulative tension in the life of the productive individual and his people; and a responsive society which gives the unusual person a feeling of purpose and allows him to breathe in an atmosphere of tolerance and humaneness.

Many of these productive circumstances, especially those which result from the total historical setting, cannot be created by special effort. Others which have to do with a society's responsiveness and liberality for example, are, at least to a considerable degree, within man's power. The United States is the one among the great Western nations which has not yet had its classical period of art and thought. This may be due to its relative youth, but it may also be due to the fact that too many of its inhabitants were not interested in the products of noble "leisure" (the term "leisure class" itself, as denoting the group of culturally working men, is characteristic of a fundamental misunderstanding of their role in civilization). There also was, and still exists, a certain lack of self-respect. Otherwise rich Americans would not have been so willing to pay thousands of dollars for sometimes mediocre paintings from abroad, while the artist at home was allowed to starve or to choose a "useful" occupation.

This situation can improve only if eventually the old dream of Noah Webster and Emerson becomes true, namely that this country develops not only a politically, but also a culturally self-conscious nation. This does not mean nationalist isolation; rather it means the harmonious combination of self-awareness and ever widening horizons which we described as essential in the birth of a classical period. Before this combination is achieved many American citizens will always oscillate between an imitative attitude laden with a strange feeling of cultural inferiority, and the compensating feeling of superiority expressing itself particularly in the pride in "democracy" and "technology."

With respect to the second circle of responsibilities to esthetic culture, namely, the things of art which surround us, this country is in a situation filled with challenge. We are now out of the age when the machine could produce only articles of cheap mass consumption. It can produce objects of real artistic value in the face of which only a snob can mind that they are no longer the precious possession of a few but can be enjoyed by many. Herewith arises one of the great cultural responsibilities of modern industry and the modern schools of applied art and industrial design. The latter have a key position in between the manufacturer and the public. They have to convince the manufacturer that his interest and prestige are better protected through esthetically more perfect forms of production and advertisement and that, in the long run, bad taste will not pay. The other task of the schools of applied art is to educate the consumer so that he becomes capable of defending himself against the continual attempt of certain types of producers to profit from the appeal to vulgarity.

But the schools of applied art should never forget that ultimately all progress in art and taste depends on the creativeness of the free artist. It is he who through his courage and imagination produces new patterns of expression. Esoteric though they may be at the beginning, if they are good, they become gradually accepted by the multitude in spite of all initial hostility and suspicion. Many of our women wear dresses with designs which betray to the trained eye the influence of painters who were laughed at thirty years ago. Without contact with the creative artist all applied art, in the course of time, becomes sterile, as a brook degenerates into a swamp when cut off from its source. However contested this statement will be: in the hierarchy of artistic values and creations all art which accepts usefulness as its primary purpose is on a level inferior to the products of imaginative and intuitional art. The reason is that the latter alone contains the element of freedom and of unhampered outflow of individuality. Through this element it inspires men and opens new vistas even to those artists who work in the sphere of application.

On the imagination of the artist depend also those among the public who enjoy esthetic experience mediately and wish to materialize the spirit of art in their own lives. They read the good books, hear the good music, and like to see and to buy masterpieces of the visual arts. They are in continual contact with the artist, and as they need him, so he needs them; for without their sympathetic response he becomes lonely and discouraged. In a society of strife and competition, and often of vulgarity, they are the bearers of the "polite" or "genteel" tradition. These words have received a somewhat snobbish flavor, but we have no reason to be proud of this achievement. On the contrary, woe to the nation where this tradition disappears. A living and pervasive tradition saves a people from barbarism through its subtle and often subconscious influence on habits and judgments much more than "moral instruction" and other weak pedagogical substitutes can ever do.

It is partly due to the utilitarian (though essentially highly unpractical) trend in education, and partly to the influx of culturally unprepared people into positions of educational importance that we lay at the present so extremely little value on a more systematic esthetic education. One can be professor at a great university and profess without shame his complete indifference to anything that belongs to art, rhythm, and beauty. Yet, in our oldest document on education, Plato's *Republic*, there is clearly emphasized the necessity of building all special instruction on a broad esthetic, or as he calls it, "musical" education. By this he means a form of schooling which (through the medium of dance and the singing of sacred hymns) conveys to the young a sense for the harmony of soul and body.

The typical modern education is one-sidedly rationalistic, with the effect that it achieves little even in the realm of the intellect; for the intellect has to be nourished by emotional impulses in order to be productive. Of the potential influence which music and rhythmical education can have on the formation and harmonization of a personality, most of our educators have no idea. But at the same time they deplore that the increase of school and the lengthening of school age has failed to have a sufficiently beneficent effect on our civilization. As if this great product of the human race, namely spiritual culture, could be achieved if more and more young people for more and more time become exposed to teachers and professors who themselves have "souls without music."

CHAPTER VI

POLITICS

INTRODUCTION

ENTERING POLITICS is like entering a wood with intertwined paths where one may easily lose his way. It may, therefore, be good to sketch, at the beginning of this chapter, a map which the reader may remember if, in the middle of the journey, he should feel himself somewhat disoriented.

We will first discuss the relationship between individual will and group will, or between individualistic-liberal attitudes and collectivistic-totalitarian attitudes toward society. Second we must attempt to arrive at some clarity with regard to the conflict between ethics and power in political life. For all political thinking and acting moves in a field where currents emanating from two opposite poles constantly cross each other; one pole represents the care for men, which is one duty of the statesman, the other pole represents power, which he has also to respect.

After understanding these fundamental problems we can deal more profitably with the great issues in modern politics; namely, with the problems of nationality and sovereignty, with the emergence of the masses, and the claims of labor.

Then we will know the kind of responsibilities facing us and will be able to imagine the principles which ought to determine future political action.

I. BASIC PROBLEMS

A. *Individualism and Collectivism*

Politics deals with individuals living in groups, and with groups consisting of individuals. This is both a fact and a profound problem. For though the co-existence between individual and group is the most fundamental requisite of human history, it is nevertheless full of friction, because the individual is often inclined to offend the laws of group life, and the group often tends to violate the happiness and productivity of the individual.

Therefore in the first part of this chapter we are going to deal with the relationship between individual and group life.

Most modern historians in democratic societies are inclined to describe human history in terms of the growing self-liberation of the individual. The enlightened thinkers of the eighteenth century challenged man, as a "rational" being, to free himself from the fetters of dull traditionalism. In contrast to the romanticists for whom tradition was something organic and necessary, like God's earth to a flower, the rationalists considered folklore, customs, mores, authority, and venerated beliefs a more or less artificial fabrication which could be changed or abandoned by acts of decision. According to some prerevolutionary French thinkers the priests and kings had always been interested in keeping the people in a state of awe and obedience; for this purpose they had to create an atmosphere of fear and superstition. In the nineteenth century philosophers such as Spencer and Comte and, in a most extreme form Nietzsche, challenged modern man to grow out of the magic of false piety and prejudices which were accepted only because people had not yet matured toward independent thinking.

No doubt, much in the criticism of tradition as an obstacle to human freedom is correct. The increasing self-assertion of the individual since the Renaissance is not merely a whim of history.

Nevertheless, it is one-sided and even dangerous to judge the behavior and history of men only from a rationalistic and individualistic point of view. Rationalist individualism, or liberalism, like all great movements in history, arrogated too quickly the role of the final arbiter of human history because it considered itself the goal and consummation.

If we want to evaluate seriously the relationship between the person and his group, we have to realize that individualism is not an absolute blessing, nor have people always been desirous of it. The really elementary impetus of history is the search for a satisfactory life. Under certain circumstances man will find this satisfaction in a high degree of absorption in the total community, its lore and the protection it offers; under other circumstances he will rejoice in a proud feeling of independence and liberty, even to the degree of arrogance. This emphasis on the desire for satisfaction as an historical agent more powerful than individualism is confirmed by the fact that in more recent times not only Russia—which has always been strongly collectivistic—has become totalitarian, but also such nations as Italy and Germany which in earlier times helped blaze the road toward individualism.

In societies exposed to physical danger the search for a satisfactory life may not go far beyond the mere struggle for survival. It always works as a strongly collectivizing element. Primitive societies stick together because only in this way can they supply food and defend themselves against wild animals, strange tribes, and supposed hostile deities. Even in highly developed societies production and war enforce cooperation and forge people together.

Furthermore there is in every individual the terrific fear of loneliness. It is imminent not only in primitive societies where seclusion from the group means physical death, but it is one of the strongest motivating factors in all human situations. For never does man discover the eternal abyss and exposure of all human existence with such a degree of anxiety as when he suddenly feels lonely. There is certainly a profound blessing in voluntary solitude—those who never can feel it are bound to become superficial—but involuntary and persistent loneliness destroys a man's health and mind.

From man's desire for communication spring all the thousandfold activities which lead him up into the sphere of culture and human refinement. Only when supply, defense, relation to the gods, and communication have achieved a certain degree of perfection, can he develop forms of satisfaction which transform him from a mere group member into an individual. For only under such conditions do individuality and temporary separation not mean the same as loneliness. If we say: "I am alone with a book," are we really? Should we not better say that we enjoy a spiritual companionship of so deep a character that foreign voices disturb our dialogue with the book in hand? But how many medieval men before the invention of the printing press could ever enjoy this delight? If they wanted to communicate with the Spirit they had either to go to wise people and talk, or to understand the art of contemplation. And this is not a popular art, today even less than in earlier times.

Thus we may say that it is largely due to environmental factors rather than to a change in mental substance that men prefer more individualistic or collectivistic modes of life.

Since the dawn of humanity when mankind discovered that there is such a thing as *cultura animi*, there always have been individuals who need a certain degree of solitude in order to unfold their inner riches. There also have been the socially favored *aristoi* with a more personal taste and desire for a noble use of leisure. But the average man in less advanced civilizations disappeared completely in the group. He could not develop the personal tastes and desires which a more friendly environment might have produced. Hence we observe in youthful periods a high degree of authoritarianism, feudal forms of social organization, ostracism and other forms of persecution against heretics.

On the other hand, under the influence of a propitious environment a relatively large number of people may develop a strong urge for individual freedom in order to find sufficient release for their desires and their initiative. Thus arose the Athenian society of the Periclean age with its "claim of excellence," its desire for "distinction," and its aversion to "constraint in private intercourse." "And we have not forgotten"—so Pericles says in his Funeral Oration—"to provide for our weary spirits many relaxations from toil; we have regular games and sacrifices throughout the year; at home the style of our life is refined; and the delight which we daily feel in all these things helps to banish melancholy. Because of the greatness of our city the fruits of the whole earth flow in upon us; so that we enjoy the goods of other countries as freely as of our own."

But that should not deceive us. Even in the most favored periods and in the most mature nations individualism never pervaded the totality of the population. It has always been a privilege of those who enjoyed the necessary power of initiative in mind and action. And they rarely were left in peace. Even in Athens, Pericles lived in constant fear of ostracism. Then there are, in prosperous times, a number of people whose tradition and wealth allow them a genteel life and education. But they would not make any sacrifices for these values. They are much more profiteers than true adepts of the individualist, or "liberal," attitude. The moment their economic privileges are endangered they can turn toward the collectivist form of fascism, just as the large industrial masses in times of crisis can become a threat to the liberal and democratic tradition.

An extreme state of insecurity always makes the majority of people, whether rich or poor, prefer safety to ideas and ideals. But the same masses can also become the voluntary guardians of democracy and liberalism if they can rely on a sound economic order. Those who like to conjure up the menace of collectivism and the proletarian revolt should keep in mind that there is no better safeguard against such dangers than common social responsibility. Freedom cannot grow on barren ground.

Perhaps we can come closer to the heart of our problem if, in addition to the historical perspective, we elaborate somewhat more the psychological side of the relationship between individualism and collectivism. Let us ask the question: To what extent has each of us in his own personality, and to what extent does each of us need for his own development, both individualist and collectivist attitudes?

Certainly it is gross exaggeration to say that there exists something like a really "independent individual." Not even the strongest individualist would deny that his well-being depends, first of all, on the degree of health and vitality which nature allows him—nature being a word for the cosmic forces which flow through us, which give us life, and in which we may envisage some inner harmony and order. The person who would try to separate himself from that embracing power would not become independent, but dead.

Secondly, our various faculties need for their development and satisfaction both communication with other people and protection. The democrat likes his system not only because it gives him a chance for the adventures of individualism, but also because it guarantees decent human relations and protects his rights.

Though a feeling of "being different" may begin in early childhood and rise to a high degree in adolescence, the full consciousness of specific individuality and of harvesting the sweet and bitter fruits from this attitude is a sign of maturity. With this comes the longing for a certain degree of being alone, the courage to deviate from the path of custom, and a personal way and color in viewing and interpreting life.

Nothing is more interesting in this respect than the study of such early Italian humanists as Petrarch and his disciples, who were the historical forerunners of modern individualism. They develop a highly personal relation to nature; landscapes are not just pleasant or unpleasant, as for medieval man, but acquire a specific mood of soul. The artists of the time create the individual human portrait, which is but a sign that the individual himself is interested in being a work of art. Readiness for the beauty, sensuousness, and even sensuality of life is no longer a shame but the mark of culture. Destiny is no longer the result of divine dispensation; instead there is the deity *Fortuna* whose whims and wills man may be able to influence by the strength of his own will and effort. In other words, idealistic indeterminism begins to replace theistic determinism. And there are mixed into the constructive trends of this period of adolescent individualism—as we may call the times of the early humanists—many great and little weaknesses, almost the same as we find among young people in the age of puberty; rapid changes from exuberant self-confidence to melancholy, and from tolerance toward intolerance; defiance of God and anxiety; vaingloriousness and self-humiliation; and hero-worship mingled with an exaggerated desire for originality.

In a way, even today we have not yet outgrown this state of contrasts. It takes the human race in its total history, as well as each individual in his own life, a long time before achieving the rational and liberal attitude which allows freedom of development and thought to one-self, and to other groups and persons. But this alone is the kind of ethical individualism which the great thinkers meant when they defended liberty against suppression, and tolerance against intolerance. They did not intend to create a robust form of self-assertion, but enrichment and enlargement of personal experience. They did not act from egotistic desire, but ultimately from the acknowledged ideal of the dignity of man. Consequently the truly developed or "liberal" individual includes into his conscience and ambitions the free development of his own ego and the liberation and progress of humanity as a whole. In other words his individualism grows into an attitude of social dignity.

Such an attitude requires firmness in basic convictions with regard to the character of humanity as much as flexibility and comprehensiveness of understanding. *Nihil humani mihi alienum est.* Because of that very complexity individualism, as all the subtle values of mankind, has difficulty defending itself against the simple logic and brutality of narrow and self-centered people. It is so much easier to believe in compact doctrines and to use one's elbows, than to combine understanding for even the strange with firmness and harmony of character.

Yet, in spite of all exposure that goes with the liberal attitude there is in it a grandeur which will be an eternal challenge to great minds in whatever political or economic frame they may be chosen, or condemned, to live. They will look with distress at the false antinomies created by one-sided individualists and collectivists, for they will know that neither from the historical, nor from the psychological point of view are collectivism and individualism mutually exclusive. Rather these represent tendencies which, though in different aggregation, occur in each person as well as in each society. The prevalence of one or the other trend will largely depend on the conditions under which a person or a society lives. In any sound person or group individualism and collectivism are compensatory factors; they become irreconcilable only if developing into extremes, and they develop into extremes only in a gravely imperiled or defective order.

To avoid such a development is one of the supreme responsibilities of politics in modern society.

B. *Politics and Power*

Politics, in its ideal sense, is the attempt at creating forms of organization through which the otherwise fortuitous social conditions and relations of men can be directed toward systematic and generally beneficial action. In so far as politics intends to regulate and improve the life of societies, both in space and in time, it is, beside education, the most embracing and responsible of all human endeavors.

As we here conceive of it, politics cannot be of merely communal or national, but must eventually be of international scope. This expansion of politics from small to wider circles corresponds not only to the growing interaction among nations, it also corresponds to a trend inherent in progressive civilizations as such. For the more developed a civilization is, the more it creates widening relations of interdependence, responsibility and, in certain cases, hostility. This width of relations in ripe civilizations is, on the one hand, a challenge and a blessing. But it can also become a task too great to be mastered by the human mind. As far as history proves there has never been a nation capable of controlling more than a small sector of this earth. Beyond a certain expanse political power has always become a chain which strangles the men who forged it.

In spite of its organizational genius, a conquering people like the Romans saw its national economy and its mores destroyed by too great an influx of new goods, ideas, and customs. The Roman citizens died on faraway battlefields while their fields at home remained unplowed or were bought by wealthy landlords. After the loss of Republican freedom a standing army of mercenaries from all over the world replaced the battalions of free men; in the course of time the generals acquired more power than the civil government, until after the second century A.D. only tryannical rulers could maintain the appearance of inner unity. The Spanish in the sixteenth, and the French in the seventeenth centuries suffered more from their expansionist ambitions than they profited from them. Nor has modern imperialism increased human happiness; not even in the country which can claim to have mastered it better and for a longer time than any other country, namely England. The international chaos of the twentieth century is not due exclusively to the sins of aggression, but also to the possessive element in imperialisms.

But it is not only our international political system that is undergoing one of the most terrific crises the world has ever seen. In most countries internal politics is in a state of utter change and disorder, because the complexity of modern life has rendered the habitual forms of economic and social organization obsolete; and so far we have not yet found solutions adequate to the new situation.

This is partly due to outright unwillingness on the part of those who profit from the chaos, partly to the lethargy and ignorance of large parts of the population, and partly also to the fact that we have never bothered to discover the essential criteria of healthy politics and to act accordingly.

In an attempt to discover these criteria, let us first guard ourselves against the sentimental confusion of politics with mere welfare and charity. Whatever the ideal goal of politics may be, in the crude atmosphere of action and reality it is the twin brother of power. And as, unfortunately, in human societies power fights power, politics is not only the noblest responsibility of the moral man, but also one of the most intensive and often most brutal forms of fighting. Hence there can be no philosophy of politics which does not grapple with the problem of power.

Because of this difficulty we possess no clear and consistent theoretical system of politics. Power is a highly unphilosophical and often unreasonable affair; it is laden with all the greatness and all the lust and crime within human capacity.

The crucial dilemma which issues from the combination of power and politics appears before us right in the first great political treatise which the Western nations possess, Plato's *Republic*. There the lawgivers and statesmen are admonished to punish the ordinary citizen who lies for his own profit, but are themselves permitted to lie if the interest of the state demands it. This doubtful permission which society gives the statesman, nay, this obligation which it imposes upon him, has kept many a worthy character away from politics. Some great statesmen such as Abraham Lincoln suffered profoundly from the moral ambiguity of their position; the majority, however, took it as an unavoidable characteristic of statesmanship and acted accordingly. Men are capable of combining many contrasts. Our modern nationalists are not aware of the fact that at home they praise deeds and ideas as signs of sound patriotism which they condemn abroad as signs of malignant chauvinism. And the geopoliticians of one country become self-righteously irritated if they suddenly discover their own neophytes growing up in other empires.

What other philosophy can underlie such an attitude but the idea that power is good if used for oneself, whereas power used by and to the advantage of the rival is evil? But how can something be good if its universal application is undesirable?

Thus man finds himself in a morass of contradictions which threaten to disturb all decent standards of international life and creep deeply even into individual ethics, for the two cannot be separated. Why wonder, then, at the "cynicism" of college youth who look through the smoke screen of propaganda and refuse to believe in the moral phrases of the older generation, though many of them may prove their patriotism and give their lives willingly for their country.

But bewilderment is today a privilege not only of academic people. Even the "common man" in the various nations has become attentive and no longer trusts all the papers and speeches about international peace, freedom, and justice in the "family of nations" who, at the same time, decided to keep for themselves the biggest resources, the biggest guns, and large colonies and "spheres of influence."

Many conscientious men would like to follow the pacifism of Christ and of Gandhi, but this radical solution conveys to them a feeling of unreality amidst a world of power. Thus they find no answer.

C. *The Dilemma of Power*

In attempting to clarify the problem of power one must first realize that power operates in most different forms for most varied purposes. It ranges almost as far as life, from the loving humility of a Francis of Assisi who certainly radiated an intense spiritual power, to the physical power of a way-layer, or the power of Napoleon.

But however much we prefer the power which is in love,

sacrifice, and freedom, to power in the sense of violence, even the most peace-loving man cannot live and thrive without making use of the latter. Spraying our trees is, in a way, an act of violence against bugs and beetles which, from a completely abstract point of view, may have the same right of feeding on the fruits of an orchard as we. But in fighting these insects few will really suffer pangs of conscience. We believe that human life has more worth than a swarm of sawflies. We also feel that human planning and labor cannot allow themselves to be destroyed by creatures whose only business seems to be to eat and reproduce.

But where is the limit for those endowed with the power of greater productivity, greater foresight and more enduring initiative? Should power, in the sense of violence, end where man meets man? This criterion seems to be right because men are essentially equal; they are in religious language all children of God and should, therefore, not be used as means or slaves in the hands of their fellow men; and they all desire a certain continuity for themselves and their offspring. But then the early American settlers would not have been justified in occupying this continent; its potential treasures would have remained unused by the one million Indians who inhabited the present territory of the United States and Canada before the advent of the early settlers. Certainly we all disapprove of the cruelty exercised by the whites in their fight against the Indians, and we are still more disgusted at the degree of religious cant used by Cotton Mather, the old Puritan preacher, who addressed the Indians with the following words:

[3] But infinitely greater was the compassion of the great God in moving the English, thus to shew you the kindness of the Lord. . . . Since you have the Gospel, the people which sat in Darkness, See a Great Light, and unto them which sat in the Region and shadow of Death, Light is sprung up. Let this goodness of God, cause you to cry out, How Good is God? and let it lead you to Repentance.[1]

[1] Cotton Mather: "An Epistle to the Christian Indians who call upon the name of Jesus Christ," Boston, 1700.

However, if we go through the propaganda literature of modern nations and examine the sermons of priests and ministers given to troops marching out to attack a foreign country or to quench seditions in suffering colonies, we will find an attitude quite similar to that of Cotton Mather.

Where is the way out of this dilemma?

It may be in the acceptance of the principle of nonviolence as recommended by Buddha, by Christ, and carried through in modern times by Gandhi and his followers. No doubt this attitude is clear, clean, and heroic. Nobody can read without admiration the description of the Vaikom incident in John S. Hoyland's *Indian Crisis*. The Vaikom incident was a test of nonviolence in the Indian movement for the emancipation of the Untouchables. As customary in India, they were forbidden to use a street in Vaikom because it led up to a temple; in addition, Brahmins inhabited the houses on both sides of the street. One day the Untouchables decided to conduct a procession up the street and were prevented by the state authorities from doing so. They insisted on their right and were jailed; more and more arrived, and they also were cast into prison. When the state prisons were full the police threw a cordon across the end of the sacred street. Gandhi, to whom the matter was referred, decided that the Untouchables had to persevere, but without violence. The only means left was to press quietly against the police cordon until the officers would give way. A large camp was established outside the town and relays of volunteers were organized who for sixteen months thronged before the police cordon, "with their heads bowed and their hands joined in the Indian attitude of prayer. . . . The rains came, the street was flooded, the police took to boats, but the volunteers stood in deep water. There was a cholera epidemic in the camp and many died. But they did not give way; and at last, in response to their unwearying *Satyagraha* (Gandhi's name for this type of passive resistance, meaning stalwart allegiance to truth), the state authorities yielded, and the procession of Untouchables marched in triumph up the street."

From the point of view of final effectiveness the religious principle of nonviolence would probably work better than all the wars and the whole mixture of threat and persuasion as customary in times of "friendly" international relations. Perhaps it would bring about the kingdom of peace, if only two or three great nations were willing to accept it in a case of conflict. Even the isolated phenomenon of conscientious objection to violence within warlike societies, as exercised by the Society of Friends, has an enormous effect on the minds of men, as the discrepancy between the actual number of Quakers and the magnitude of their influence shows sufficiently. They represent the living conscience of mankind.[2]

Nevertheless it is idle to dream of the acceptance of *Satyagraha* by the bearers of political power. The Indian virtues of pity, self-sacrifice, harmlessness, and conquest of selfish desire, or the Christian virtues of love and charity, though praised in books and recommended to "the masses," are considered suicidal by those who rule.

Thus those who cannot decide in favor of the principle of nonviolence and who, on the other hand, hate violence as a principle, will have to seek a form of power which reduces external force and coercion to a minimum and places itself in the service of humanly productive purposes. This is a compromise, and nobody can say that it is good enough to give the human soul peace and harmony. For there will always be the danger of the hypocritical attitude of a Cotton Mather, there will always be innumerable excuses for selfish expansions, and there will be thousands of occasions when leaders of nations will tell their people to defend their sacred rights while in reality they are invited to destroy the sacred rights of others. The older Christian theologians described man and his governments as a battleground between the demons of the devil and the angels of God. They were, in spite of their magic symbolism in the explanation of

[2] See also: Krishnalal Shridarani, *War Without Violence* (New York: Harcourt, Brace and Co., 1939).

hereditary sin, certainly more realistic than a type of modern liberal who constantly speaks of progress as if, by some kind of divine predestination, it were bound to fall like a ripe orange into our laps. A much more effective morality could be built on the courageous admission of failure than on its denial, which is often nothing more than a surreptitious form of escape.

Of course, all depends on the spirit in which we confess our fault. If it leads to hopeless and desperate feelings of guilt then it is the beginning of inertia, social neuroses, and often also of political tyranny. If, on the other hand, the knowledge of our guilt leads toward a realistic appraisal of the defects of human life, and strengthens our will to fight evils, then it is the best and the only means of reform.

But one may nevertheless ask for more stable criteria in the use of power than just the good intention to apply it wisely. With power being what it is, are we not condemned to relativism and self-deception? The answer is: We may fall into these errors, but we are not bound to do so. Even in the ambiguous situation where we may decide for coercion, we will always have to ask ourselves whether we do so out of the desire for profit, whether for ourselves and for our country only, or whether we are motivated by a higher principle which can be applied to humanity as a whole. And if we are in need of a more definite concept, no measure can serve better as a check on our deeds of power than the criterion as to whether we have a goal at the end of our intentions which reflects the idea of freedom—not only for us, but also for those we expose to temporary coercion—or whether we strive for a goal which contains suppression and exploitation as an inherent element. If we accept this criterion then those who use power rightly would feel like good parents or teachers whose aim it will always be to use their influence for gradually rendering themselves superfluous.

To express the same idea in other words: we are here confronted with a "dialectical" situation, as is the case with almost every complex and profound problem of life. A man is in a dialectical situation when he is exposed to conflicts and contrasts, but at the same time feels compelled to solve the dilemma on a higher plane of thought and action. The higher plane toward which those who use power would have to strive can be expressed in many different terms which, nevertheless, all mean the same thing. Call it, if you will, a higher degree of creativeness in an atmosphere of confidence and sharing, not only with respect to those who exercise power, but also to those to whom it is applied. Or call it the recognition of the freedom and dignity of the fellow man which challenges you to grant him the same cultural conditions you would consider essential for yourself and your children. Or use the New Testament's idea of *Agápe*, or charity, or love, and think that the same Christ who gave the word love its fullest meaning, said to his followers: "I give you power." In all humble awareness of your imperfection seek to change the brutal concept of power into the concept of practical and spiritual brotherhood—these are the higher principles of thought and action which could place the constructive elements in power above the destructive ones.

Whenever in the course of human events societies forget the ethical challenge inherent in power and enjoy it merely for the sake of self-aggrandizement, they endanger their own future. History, not today or tomorrow but in its eternity, is the undeceivable arbiter of human action. It is cruel, in that it often punishes not the evil-doers, but "the third and fourth generations." Yet it is just. To be sure, there are many who do not mind what will happen with their own or other people's children if only they themselves can die in wealth. These men, whether so-called respectable people or not, are the scum of mankind. And unfortunately, there has always been much of it. But power will always challenge the conscience of those who have a stronger sense for humanity.

Whether the sympathies of such people are more on the side of complete nonviolence, or whether they hold the wise use of power to be inevitable in national and international contacts, they will suffer from the iniquities of political rivalry. But rather than suffer passively, they will have to throw their energy into the cruel relativity of life to make it as little cruel as possible. They will try to alter power increasingly from an instrument of brutality to an instrument of prudence and voluntary co-operation. This is the only way to make civilization and power relatively compatible. Completely compatible they never will be.

The attempt at matching power and civilization makes the statesman responsible for the provision of all those basic conditions of healthy human life which we have discussed in the previous chapters of this book. Only that kind of politics is productive which helps men to provide food and work, allows them to use their reason and develop faith, gives them a vision of excellence and an opportunity to share their joys and their sufferings, and provides conditions under which they can develop their personal qualities in the service of purposes adequate to both their individual talents and the moral demands of human society. Thomas Hobbes is right when he says in the tenth chapter of his treatise *De Homine* that politics is akin to ethics, in that it is "the knowledge of the just and the unjust, of the right and the wrong . . . because we human beings have made laws and treaties according to the principle which we have recognized as corresponding to the just and the right as contrasted to the unjust and the wrong, in other words as the causes of justice." [3]

A moral law, one of the few to be found in all cultures whether primitive or complicated, forbids the murder of members of the same ingroup, but no code, no custom, and no legislation have so far succeeded in eliminating the exploitation of the weaker by the stronger even within the same group. Slavery has been an acknowledged institution even in highly developed civilizations, though the slaves were preferably taken from an outgroup. The treatment of women, up

[3] Thomas Hobbes, "De Homine," *Opera Philosophica*, Vol. II (London: 1839).

to modern times, was often nothing but another form of slavery. The lack of conscience which so-called gentlemen with high standards of decency among their equals showed in their treatment of less fortunate classes within their own nation is such that one cannot wonder at the wild revolutionary outbreaks occurring in every century of our civilization. But in spite of these warnings, every step taken by governments or by self-help organizations toward securing a minimum of public welfare was violently opposed by a considerable number of the potent under some kind of ideological disguise. Only in some few countries co-operative tendencies begin to replace authoritarian sentiments of employers in relation to their employees.

Naturally, the sins of omission and commission are incomparably greater in the relationship between ingroups and outgroups. For centuries and centuries powerful nations have destroyed recklessly the liberty of the powerless; the particular standards of the subjected peoples were demolished, partly in order to eliminate undesirable opposition, partly also out of sheer stupidity about indigenous values and achievements in foreign nations. Often opposition could have been changed into co-operation if the self-imposed masters had realized that power diminishes its effect the more it relies on physical force, whereas it increases its influence if it turns toward humaneness and understanding. But the insight into this fact is identical with the acknowledgement that, in the long run, man profits more from sharing than from competition and organized stealing. Though this insight has gradually grown in individuals, it will still take some time before it becomes a living reality among nations.

The hostility between conquering and conquered groups always grew when there was at stake a fight between so-called superior and inferior races. As during the past four hundred years it was particularly the white race that possessed more effectual means of conquest than other races, Western civilization was given a great opportunity to prove its moral substance. We cannot know how the other races of the earth

would have behaved had they been given a similar chance.
However, the moral record of the white race can cause no
other group on earth to bow in admiration. Let us say in plain
words: "It is shameful." Lip service, of course, was paid *ad
nauseam* to the ideals of humanity: Article twenty-two of the
Covenant of the League of Nations, which deals with "man-
datory territories," or the former German colonies and some
Turkish dependencies, explains the willingness of the victorious nations of the first World War to take over the burden
of new responsibilities in the following terms:

To those colonies and territories which as a consequence of the late
war have ceased to be under the sovereignty of the States which for-
merly governed them and which are inhabited by peoples not yet able
to stand to themselves under the strenuous conditions of the modern
world, there should be applied the principle that the well-being and
development of such peoples form a sacred trust of civilization and
that securities for the performance of this trust should be embodied in
this Covenant.

The best method of giving practical effect to this principle is that
the tutelage of such peoples should be entrusted to advanced nations
who by reason of their resources, their experience, or their geographical position can best undertake this responsibility, and who are willing
to accept it, and that this tutelage should be exercised by them as
Mandatories on behalf of the League.[4]

In earlier times a treaty, mostly enforced by one victorious
nation on another, began by conjuring the name of the "Al-
mighty" or the "Holy Trinity." In modern times reference
to a great humanitarian mission of the nations with the bigger
armies is being considered more attractive. Whether the appeal to God or the appeal to a cultural mission is more offensive is difficult to decide. However, the fact is that in one of
the few cases where great nations would really have performed a cultural mission, namely, in quickly suppressing
the gangsterism of Mussolini and Hitler through the simple

[4] Michael Demiashkevich, *Shackled Diplomacy, The Permanent Factors of
Foreign Policies of Nations* (New York: Barnes and Noble, 1934), p. 69.

and bloodless form of total economic and political boycott, these powers as well as great firms and rich individuals within these nations, preferred a deal with them. They even helped to finance the enterprises of Mussolini and Hitler until they discovered that fascism was not only a means of suppressing the trade-unions, "the cultural menace of Bolshevism," and the welfare of "minor" nations, but that it imperiled also the vital interests of the big nations and big business themselves.

II. The Great Issues in Modern Politics

There are three great and immediate tasks which the future bearers of power will have to master if they wish to have world civilization instead of world tyranny. Any political organization that wishes different national or ethnic groups to co-operate peacefully will have to cope with the tendency toward national self-assertion or self-determination on the part of national minorities, or—to say it in one word—with nationality. Furthermore, the future bearers of power will have to reckon with the emergence of the masses as a co-determining factor in politics and economics, and they will have to incorporate in one way or another the claim of labor toward partnership in the modern industrial process. We shall discuss now each of these trends in somewhat more detail.

A. Nationality

1. *The Dual Character of Nationalism*

The urge toward national self-determination, or the feeling of nationality, represents that stage of development in the life of a social group in which it becomes proudly conscious of its common cultural heritage. Such a group considers itself distinguished from other groups by its specific folklore, often also by its specific religious tradition, and most of all by its language even though sometimes one or the other of these characteristics does not apply. Only community of language seems to be indispensable. When this historical stage of self-consciousness and feeling of uniqueness is reached such national groups which have not yet achieved a government of their own but are subjected to foreign rule, violently aspire to political independence. They hold that they, and nobody else, has the right to be master of their national destiny. This desire can grow to such a degree that men and women are willing to sacrifice any other interest on the altar of their people's sovereignty. Those who have ever felt their nationality suppressed will understand these sentiments.

Yet, there is a big debit beside the credit account in the ledger of nationality. It has not only helped to ruin empires which were probably ripe to fall such as those of the Ottomans and the Romanovs, but also the older Austrian multinational state which fulfilled a historical mission. For however much we may criticize the rule of the Hapsburgs and the defectiveness of their nationalities policy, there can be no doubt that the population under the old Danube monarchy was, on the whole, happier than it was after its destruction. The exaggerated emphasis on national rights has caused people to hate each other who with a more balanced attitude could have lived in peace; thus it worked toward the fragmentation of modern mankind. Nationalism has prevented the modern world from developing sound national economics within a sound international economy, adequate to the modern means of traffic and production. This is perhaps the greatest damage which the rigid principle of nationality has inflicted on the modern nations.

In addition, nationalism has never been consequent. Rather than being a medium of liberation, it was often confused with imperialistic tendencies on the part of the stronger power and used for the suppression of unpleasant minorities. Every historian could easily quote from political leaders in all the great countries statements which are saturated with nationalist arrogance; unfortunately, this spirit is as appealing to the members of the same group as it is repelling to other groups.

Attacks on peaceful nations have been defended with reference to the sacred mission of the more powerful nation; myths of superiority and inferiority have been created and have served to provide an undisturbed conscience to the most brutal exploiters and persecutors of other races; and in the name of the cultural mission of the white man, "backward" ethnic groups have been submitted to cures during which the physician waxed fat and the patient grew weaker, even to the degree of extirpation or degeneration.

But in spite of the conflicts presented by modern nationality it would be meaningless to condemn it as a merely dangerous force which historical progress ought to eliminate as soon as possible. Rather we have to ask more exactly: where are the positive and the negative qualities in nationality, and has politics available means which would reduce the latter to a minimum?

For answering this question we may venture a brief historical analysis.

The passionateness of nationalist feelings which in modern times seem to have replaced the religious fanaticism of earlier periods, could make us assume that nationalism is a deeply ingrained and perennial instinct of man. As a matter of fact, a group obsessed by the passion of nationalism is inclined to imbue such a belief into the minds of its members and to ostracize everybody who refuses to share it. But only a slight knowledge of history proves that periods of great achievement, such as the Middle Ages, accomplished their unique contribution to civilization not through the cultivation of separatist nationalism, but through their belief in ideas of universal character. As we already stated in our historical chapter, we would not have any Western civilization—whatever it is worth—without the gigantic attempt of medieval man to integrate the competing tribes, peoples, and cultures into one great body with a common religion for all and a supernational language for the literati.

Yet, the professed universalist attitude of the Middle Ages must not blur our judgment of the feelings of the majority about whom we have no historical record. Almost everything laid down in medieval books was written by members of the clergy, who adhered to a supernational philosophy of history. From these sources we learn little about the broad currents of lay mentality. However, we know that intense national feelings sometimes flared up in nations attacked by foreign powers. When the Germans in the battle of Liegnitz stemmed the tide of the Mongol invaders into Europe, when the Italian cities defended themselves against Frederick Barbarossa, when the French followed Jeanne d'Arc into the battles against the English, they certainly were inspired by nationalist sentiments. Signs of profound national attachment can also be found in the great epics and knightly songs of the time. Yet on the scale of medieval values nationality was not as high up as it is today, and as it was long before the Middle Ages.

The ancient Jews, for example, became a nation through the belief in their special covenant with the Lord.[5] "For thou art an holy people unto the Lord thy God, and the Lord has chosen thee to be a peculiar people unto Himself, out of all the nations that are upon the earth." In this one sentence is indicated the fate of the Jewish people: to be and remain a spiritual community in spite of living in the diaspora, and to fulfill God's will, or to bear his punishment for disobedience, until all the peoples on the earth shall harken to His word.

The grandeur of the civilization of the Greeks was interlinked with their pride in their national language and tradition. It caused them, like the Jews, to despise all other peoples as barbarians with no righteous claim for the dignity they possessed themselves.

Different from Hebrew and Greek nationalism of the "chosen-people" sort was Roman imperialism. Growing out of intense patriotism, it nevertheless left room for the acknowledgment of gods, languages, and customs outside the nation, mainly because with growing conquests, and at a rela-

[5] See in this connection: Hans Kohn, *The Idea of Nationalism, A Study in its Origins and Background* (New York: Macmillan and Co., 1944).

tively early stage of their national development, the Romans met the undeniably superior cultures of Greece, Asia, and Africa. The Pax Romana, consequently, represents a mixture of political imperialism and cultural pluralism.

Generally the modern imperialist nations have not followed the Roman example in respecting the culture of subjected nations. To be sure, except under the perversive influence of Hitlerism the citizens of white nations have considered it good standard to conceal the strange and completely irrational feeling of pride which they derive from belonging to their specific nation. After all, it is not anyone's merit or fault to belong to one or the other nationality. But in dealing with other races, especially with colonial peoples, the Western nations have failed to achieve the broadness and universality of mind characteristic of the enlightened men of late Antiquity.

Modern nationalism, unfortunately, resembles more the Hebrew and the Greek, than the Roman type. The conception of a nation as a unique symbol of civilization emerges distinctly in the political and educational literature of the Renaissance. The humanists wanted the younger generation educated not only for the life beyond and for the universal ideas of Christianity, but also for practical citizenship. The vocabulary used for denoting the goals of education changed: it no longer overflowed with such medieval terms as "humility," "being an alien on this earth," and "preparation for eternal life." Rather there appeared such terms as "glory," "deserving fame in the service of one's country and his prince," and "becoming a good soldier and diplomat."

The next steps in the growth of nationalism were the English revolution of 1648 and the French revolution of 1789. In these revolutions more than in any dynastic war the fighting nation was inspired by a feeling of unity, and each member felt himself responsible for the future of his people. The *levée en masse* of the year 1793 was the first signal of modern total warfare which replaced the relatively small armies of professional soldiers by armies of the people. The last great combination of a successful civil war of the masses with a military *levée en masse* against foreign enemies was the Russian revolution of 1917. It is significant that in each of these revolutions nothing helped so much to inspire the revolutionary groups as the aggression from outside; it added the strength of nationalist sentiments to the revolutionary fervor. In all likelihood each of the three revolutions would have developed differently had the stimulus of outside interference been lacking.

But the four historical steps toward nationalism, the Renaissance, the English, the French, and the Russian revolutions, were not only political events in the narrow sense of the word. As all great historical phenomena, they were also of profound psychological nature. In the Renaissance arose modern individualism, expressed religiously in Luther's and Calvin's forms of Protestantism; the English and the French revolutions transferred this individualism from the personal to the political realm in that they generated the modern concept of the citizen; and the Russian revolution brought about the transition of the masses from czarist theocracy toward a party state of communist character which, through its emphasis on education and co-operation, also may contain democratic elements.

In all the modern revolutions since the seventeenth century a powerful dynamic worked away from older dynasticism, for which the welfare of the monarchical house rather than that of the nation was the supreme law, toward nationality represented by the totality of free and patriotic citizens. Similar trends could be shown also in other countries which went through the historical conflict between autocratic governments of divine sanction to government by the people. All this proves that nationality, or the urge toward national self-determination, is in the life of the states nothing but the historical parallel to the growing desire for individual self-determination which we could observe as a determining factor in Western societies since the period of the Renaissance. Nationality is individualism, writ large, or the identification of the self-conscious modern personality with his political group whereby this group as such receives the same attributes of personality and dignity which the individual claims for himself. Hence it could happen, and was bound to happen, that the liberal movements of the eighteenth and nineteenth centuries carried not only the banner of personal freedom and the "natural rights of man" but also the banner of nationality.

Even when in the second half of the nineteenth century monarchs and monarchists like Napoleon III, William I of Germany and his chancellor Bismarck, Victor Emannuel II of Sardinia and his minister Cavour, and the czars Alexander II and Alexander III took away the political impetus from bourgeois liberalism and began the reorganization of Europe from above with the help of their armies, they had to compromise between the old dynastic principle of monarchical legitimacy and the new principle of nationality. Though they disliked it, they had to pay respect in order to secure the necessary public support for their governments.

Finally paragraph fourteen of Wilson's Fourteen Points, which demands national self-determination, represents but a further expression of the whole trend toward nationality issuing from the Renaissance and the Enlightenment, inspiring the great bourgeois revolutions and accepted, to a degree, even by monarchies.

But new trends and ideals are always cut across and prevented from full development by the hang-overs from older periods of civilization.

Thus for hundreds of years after the Renaissance dynastic marriages and wars decided the fate of whole groups of population. Against the most fundamental ideas of Protestant individualism, the Diet of Augsburg, in 1555, consecrated the principle *cuius regio, eius religio*. According to this most humiliating of the many political expediencies appearing in the wake of the Reformation, the subjects of a prince had to accept his religion, which meant that certain German principalities were thrown into a state of continual unrest.

Also in the treaty of Versailles in 1918 Wilson's endeavor failed to a large extent, for it was applied only in favor of the enemies of the Germans, while the German claims were disregarded. Yet, the attention given all over the world to Wilson's Fourteen Points, and the chaos which arose from their one-sided application, prove the effect of the principle of nationality on the minds of men. For the purpose of propaganda even a Hitler had to give lip service to it. In his Reichstag address of May 21, 1935 he declared:

Our racial theory regards every war for the subjection and domination of an alien people as a proceeding which sooner or later changes or weakens the victor internally, and eventually brings about his defeat. But we do not believe for a moment that in Europe the nations whose nationalism has been completely consolidated could in the era of the principle of nationalities be deprived of their national birthright at all.[6]

The irony of history destined this man who rode the crest of the waves of nationalism to break down because he offended his own dogma in his relations with other nations.

2. *The Two Levels of Sovereignty*

But why could so natural and necessary a historical trend as that of nationality work so disruptively as it did?

In our discussion of the relationship between individualism and collectivism we saw that the exaggeration of either of these two trends at the expense of the other offends the natural order of human society. So also nationality, which we explained earlier as an expansion of the individualistic principle into the life of nations, must acknowledge, besides itself, the collective side of life; namely, the co-operation among different nations.

In the relation between individuals freedom is possible and meaningful only if it operates within a framework which

[6] Adolf Hitler, *Speech Delivered in the Reichstag*, May 21, 1935. Approved Translation. (Berlin: W. Müller und Sohn, 1935.)

gives the free actions of various individuals a common purpose. So also the desire for freedom of nationality can unfold its productive qualities only if the different nations, in spite of all differences, are united by some common purpose. Wilson foresaw this dimly when, as a countercheck to the principle of national autonomy, he advocated the League of Nations. Unfortunately, the actual result of his initiative was only a parody of the hopes of mankind.

But was it only the malice of shortsighted statesmen which prevented the League of Nations from operating successfully? One has only to read the memoirs of Viscount Robert Cecil to understand how much malice and shortsightedness there was. But why could they be so dominant? It was mainly that the statesmen of 1918 and after could not find a combination between the principle of nationality and the necessity of international co-operation. They were incapable of creating political unity of supernational character which could check the evil and protect the justified claims of nationality.

In order to find such a combination one must distinguish between two levels of national sovereignty—the term sovereignty being used here as the practical political expression of national self-determination.

In the course of human progress—when and wherever there is any—the individual has learned to carve out a sphere of freedom which he has identified with his own personal dignity. Since in the American tradition this sphere of freedom and dignity has been called "the natural rights" we will use this term here, though from a merely scholarly point of view one may doubt the eighteenth century theory of "natural law."

The American Constitution refers especially to the freedom of speech, of the press, of property, of the right to petition, and trial by jury. But Franklin and Jefferson would probably have admitted that these are partly based on, and have partly to be complemented by, the conditions which according to our previous considerations constitute human civilization; namely, the opportunity to feed and shelter one-self, to work, to improve one's standards, to reason, to be-lieve, and to share. To those must be added the conditions of sound psychological growth. In turn, the realization of these rights is contingent upon man's language as the most per-sonal means of communication, upon religion as the matrix of beliefs and values, on education as the means for their tradition and continual renewal, and the mores and customs in which the various forms of communication, beliefs, values, and education find their mold. Consequently these elements have also to be included in the "natural rights." All these values we may call here the internal conditions, or the *interna* of a sound and full life.

Any national or ethnic group will wish this whole body of "natural rights" or *interna* respected by outsiders. If these rights are willfully oppressed or interfered with, the group feels its cultural self-determination jeopardized and runs sooner or later into a state of rebellion. In other words: here man and his group must be sovereign.

Outside this sphere are what we may call the *externa* of life, or the practical and technical interests of society, the purpose of which is to provide most effectively the greatest welfare for the greatest mass of the people. Thus these change according to the principle of efficiency and to the particular requirements of a historical situation. One could say that the *interna* have to be appreciated as ends in them-selves, whereas the *externa* are means; and whereas men have the right to be insistent about ends, there ought to be nothing dogmatic about the means, provided they are decent. To be sure, their execution has a great significance with re-spect to the *interna* or "natural rights." It helps or impedes their proper implementation and, most of all, makes possible the development of useful purpose without which, as we saw, the inner life of man can find no hold in the outer world.

To the sphere of the *externa* belongs the formal side of all organizations and administrations, to it belongs also the economic system, or the ways in which the problems of production and distribution are handled. To the external sphere belong, furthermore, transportation, tariffs, and the utilization of natural resources for the good of the nation and the common good of mankind—briefly all these sections of human life where people meet to arrange the business of human existence in such a way that it does not disturb, but promotes the happiness of men.

With this distinction between the *interna* and the *externa* we have indicated the two levels of sovereignty. The *interna* are, so to speak, the soul of the people, the others are pragmatical and functional. Therefore, whenever nations meet nations, or majorities meet minorities, or bigger powers smaller powers with the purpose of exercising influence, such contact will work only if they distinguish carefully between the internal and the external spheres in the life of the other group. If a group feels that its internal life is respected, it will be willing to discuss and accept co-operation and even some pressure in the area of externals. If, on the other hand, the *interna* are disregarded, not even the most skillful management and persuasion, and still less the application of power, can create peace and confidence.

Hence, whenever peoples deal with the great problem of constructing international peace either they will respect these principles and will succeed, or they will tinker around with partial and surface problems and again fail. No physician will ever succeed who sees only the symptoms and not the causes of the reactions of the human soul and body.

Transferred from theoretical to practical politics the principle just expounded would mean that diverse national groups can organize into greater unities only if the policy of "cultural sovereignty" or "cultural autonomy" is reckoned within the new communal boundaries. This policy would imply the following methods: On the one hand, all small national or ethnical groups would have full freedom with respect to their *interna*, i.e. language, religion, mores, and schools, provided they conformed to the general standards of humanity. On the other hand, the practical side of human life, or the *externa*, would be regulated in flexible and functional relation to its specific conditions. Small units and regions might be established if this is the most appropriate way, as might be the case with certain future forms of manufacturing. There may be big units of the size of whole unified territories or whole continents, as is likely to be done in regulating international problems of traffic, exchange of goods, defense, and diplomatic representation.

The same principle of functionality would have to prevail with respect to specific systems of economy. If in one country the majority of the people fare better with a more capitalistic system, let them have it. If in another country a more collectivistic and state centralized system works better, why not apply it? The test in these fields lies not in theories and preconceived principles, however coherent and logical they may appear in abstraction, but in greater efficiency.

This principle will have to be applied first in Europe— if that continent is not to remain a vale of suffering and decay.

3. *The Dismal Record and Attempts at a Solution*

When reviewing the political and cultural contacts between nations with assumedly different interests, between majorities and minorities, and between technically more advanced and technically less developed civilizations one can only be amazed at the amount of ignorance and lack of respect for the most fundamental conditions of international contact as we tried to develop them.

But instead of talking about the false use of power in general, let us give a few examples of the methods in which, in recent decades, the problem of nationality was handled by responsible powers.

When, before 1913, the Prussian government tried to Germanize the Polish minorities in the eastern part of its realm, they improved the economic conditions of the Polish worker and peasant which, in itself, was no great accomplishment considering the exploitation of the poor man in Poland by his own landlords and capitalists. Yet, at the same time the Prussian government tried to suppress the Polish language in school and interfered in the Catholic religious instruction and worship. The result was not Germanization but an increase of hostility on the part of the Polish population and its extremely influential clergy.

Forcing Germany, which had just accepted a democratic government, to confess herself exclusively responsible for the war was the gravest mistake of the Versailles Treaty. The enforcement of the war-guilt clause more than the defeat as such, the loss of Alsace-Lorraine and other territories, the occupation, the war debts, and the inflation, gave Hitler the opportunity to intensify the fever which burns in the blood of every defeated nation and to make the Germans cynical about democracy. The external political and economic compensations, taken by a victorious from a defeated nation, would have been understood, and their exaggeration could have been rectified in the course of time. But the war-guilt clause hit the center of the sick soul of the people as a whole; it offended the sphere which we called the *interna*. In addition, everybody knew that it was a hypocritical measure.

After 1918 the Italians were given certain Austrian parts of the Tyrol, and in October 1920, in contrast to the spirit of the Fourteen Points, the Austrians of German stock in this part of the Tyrol were declared to be Italians without being granted the right of plebiscite. The more reconciliatory policy tried by liberal Italian governments after 1920 met from the beginning the determined resistance of the Italian population of the Trentino and was too weak to overcome this opposition. After Mussolini had come to power he declared in a speech of February 6, 1926, in the Chamber of Deputies, that the Germans in Alto Adige did not represent a minority but only an "ethnical relic," though the Italian census in 1921 had resulted in the following numbers:

Germans	193,350
(according to German estimates 212,500)	
Italians	20,976
Ladins	11,694
Foreign Population......	24,516

The German language, the memories of the German past of thousands of years were suppressed, and public buildings could not be erected in the traditional style of the Tyrol but had to be built in the neo-Roman style. A royal decretal of January 11, 1926 ordered the change of all such family names into Italian which betrayed German or Ladin origin. Children were pressed to join the Fascist youth organizations even against the will of their parents. The nostrification of degrees acquired at foreign universities was refused and Italian religious instruction was introduced in all schools of the country. The Italian prefect of the German city of Bozen gave the order that the German names on gravestones had to be Italianized or effaced, and when this measure did not work all applications for renewal of "leases" of burial grounds were refused.[7]

Can one wonder that under these circumstances the nationalism of the Austrians who observed the suffering of their former compatriots grew to the point of seething in spite of all "treaties" between Mussolini and the Austrian chancellors who had to choose between the Italian and the German dictators? When finally the paradoxy of international politics, over the dead body of Austria, forged Hitler and Mussolini together, there was no other way to give a glimmering of security to the new pact of friendship but to remove the Germans in the Italian South Tyrol from their farms and towns.

[7] Chmelar, J., *National Minorities in Central Europe*. Prague, 1937; Amende, Ewald. *Die Nationalitaeten in den Staaten Europas. Samlung von Lageberichten*. Herausgegeben im Auftrage des Europäischen Nationalitäten Kongresses. Wien, 1931; *The Case of German South Tyrol against Italy*. Translated from *Die Wahrheit über Südtirol* by C. H. Herford. London, 1927.

Most of them were told to begin farming in Hitler's newly conquered territory of Poland where destiny awaited them with new surprises.

This degradation of human beings into the role of cattle is a sin committed by all great nations. The behavior of the French, the English, and other colonizing nations in their possessions in Africa or Asia, sometimes inhabited by highly civilized people, is also a story of shame and horror.

No doubt, the consummation of inhuman tactics, at least in Europe, has been achieved by Hitler and his satellites. And, most unfortunately, the old wisdom holds true again that at the end of a protracted and cruel war the aggressors and the defenders, the victors and the defeated, are liable to use the same methods. It may be that the self-destruction of Western civilization will continue—but now with the involuntary help of democracies which no longer understand themselves and their purposes; which were strong enough to defeat Nazism by dint of arms, but are not strong enough to set the great aim of a new and practical social humanism against the collectivism of misery which appears in many parts of our world of potential plenty. It will take generations before Europe overcomes the hatred planted by this most recent relapse into barbarism.

But it may also lead to global conflicts more destructive than even the second World War, if the white race as a whole does not place its policy in foreign continents on a clear distinction between the inner sovereignty of man and the technical sphere of international communication. It took the white race only slightly more than a hundred years to change its economy from rather primitive forms of industry and agriculture toward modern mechanized production. The Chinese and the Indians can learn this in shorter time, because the thinking and the inventing have already been done —just as the Japanese profited from Western science. Such great peoples of the East as the Indians, despite all contrary efforts of certain Western nations, will not only go on in their attempts at liberation, but will enforce the exploitation of their enormous resources in metals, known to exist but still buried in the earth, and wrest the industry in their own country more and more out of foreign hands. They may ally themselves in one way or another with Russian bolshevism. Should there be more wars they may be the most decisive factor, for they are superior not only in manpower, but also in the capacity for living on small amounts of food although science may eliminate the importance of manpower in war.

In other words, if the present conditions in the contact between West and East prevail, then it requires no political astronomy to foresee wars of greater parts of Asia against white nations; and after they are over, the "white man's burden" will certainly no longer press his shoulders. He will be his own burden.

With much justification from a moral point of view the Western nations condemned the cruelties of the Russian bolshevist revolution of 1917. It ought to be somewhat embarrassing for these nations that, at least within its boundaries before 1939, the Soviet Republic has chosen by far the most human and consequently by far the most effective way of dealing with the problem of nationality.[8] It has done so in accordance with the old demand of socialism to grant to minorities the right of self-determination.

The Russian bolshevists found themselves in a situation different from countries with colonial possessions or annexions of former enemy territories. Russia's various nationalities live in one geographical whole. The loss of the western provinces after the first World War freed the Bolshevists from the nationalities most difficult to appease, notably the Poles. "Except for the Great Russians who constituted up to 1939 some fifty-two per cent of the total population of the Soviet Union, only the Ukrainians number more than twenty per cent." The other minorities—which amount to about 138

[8] See esp. the excellent analysis of Soviet Nationalities Policy in an article by Erich Hula: "The Nationalities Policy of the Soviet Union. Theory and Practice," *Social Research*, May 1944.

different ethnic groups—"are hardly more than splinters, with little, if any, political weight of their own." [9] They had neither the intention nor the power to secede. Thus the missionary spirit of bolshevism could be confident to overcome the danger of separation by pursuing a combined policy, namely, administrative and economic centralization under the government of the Communist party, together with the policy of cultural self-determination of the different ethnical minorities. In the Soviet Republics legal equality was established among different races of the Union and all nationalities were represented with equal rights in the Council of Nationalities. Backward tribes received better education on the basis of the assumption that they could profit from learning as much as any other part of the population. Land was restored to natives with long-term credits and improved means for agricultural production. Native languages were not repressed but cultivated, and ethnological museums and institutes were founded for encouraging the study of national backgrounds. New alphabets were invented to give natives with undeveloped literature the opportunities for international communication. The Latin alphabet was substituted for the Arabic one and other reforms were carried on among the Islamic Russians, particularly with respect to the role of women.[10]

All this was not achieved wthout intensive struggle within the Communist party itself. In Lenin's Concluding Speech at the eighth Congress of the Russian Communist Party, delivered on March 19, 1919 we read:

. . . It seems to me that the Finnish example and that of the Bashkirs show that in the question of nationality it is not possible to proceed from the assumption that economic unity is necessary at any price. Necessary, of course, it is. But we must attain it through propaganda, through agitation, through a voluntary union. The Bashkirs distrust the Russians, because the Russians are at a higher level of civi-

[9] E. Hula, *op. cit.*, p. 185.
[10] S. S. Stavrianos, "Minority Rights in Russia," *Canadian Forum*, Vol. XVI, Nov. 1936, pp. 6-8.

lization and have used their civilization to rob the Bashkirs. Consequently in these remote districts the name Russian means "oppressor" to the Bashkirs, . . . We must take that into account, we must combat it. But that takes a long time. It is not to be got rid of by a decree. We must go to work on this very cautiously. Above all such a nation as the Russians, who have excited a wild hatred in all other nations, must be particularly cautious. We have only now learned to manage better, and even that only some of us as yet. Thus there are Communists among us who say "uniform schools," and accordingly no instruction to be given except through the Russian language. In my view a Communist who thinks in this way is a pan-Russian chauvinist. This tendency still exists in many of us, and we must wrestle with it.

Consequently we must say to the other peoples that we are internationalists through and through, and are striving for a voluntary union of the workers and peasants of all nations. That does not by any means rule out wars. War is another question, following from the nature of Imperialism. If we are to fight Wilson, and Wilson turns a small nation into his tool, then we shall fight against this tool. . . . Under certain conditions a war may appear inevitable. But in the question of self-determination the position is that the various peoples proceed along the same historic course, but by very different circuitous routes and paths, and that nations at a higher level of civilization proceed of set purpose in a different way to those at a lower level. . . . If we were to leave this out of sight, we should be cutting the nationality question out of our programme. We could do so if men had no national characteristics. But men of that sort do not exist, and we can build up a Socialist society in no other way.[11]

Similar discussions reoccur constantly in the manifestoes of the Communist party. The second Congress of the Communist International declared in July 1920:

". . .3. The imperialistic war of 1914–1918, waged by both sides with the slogan of the liberation of peoples and the right of peoples to self-determination, has made thoroughly clear to all peoples and to the oppressed classes of the whole earth the mendacity of bourgeois democratic phrasemaking. This war has shown by the peace treaties of

[11] Hans Kohn, *Nationalism in the Soviet Union* (London: G. Routledge & Sons, Ltd., 1933), Appendix I, pp. 135-37.

Brest-Litovsk and Bucharest on the one hand and of Versailles and St. Germain on the other how the victorious bourgeoisie has quite shamelessly fixed the national boundaries to its own economic advantage." [12]

In the course of time the following philosophy of nationalities seems to have emerged among the Soviets. They believe that both economic and political developments are bound to lead the world toward a communist form of internationalism which will even have an international language. As Stalin phrases it, he believes in "the fusion of the national cultures into one (formally and intrinsically) uniform culture with a common language." [13] But this does not exclude "the flowering of cultures national in form and Socialist in content under the dictatorship of the proletariat in a country." Nor does it exclude the coexistence of different national cultures within the family of nations. The future world international, according to the Bolshevists, can be communist and multinational at once.

Whatever one thinks about Russian Communism, it has astonished the world by its unity and power of resistance against the German attack in the second World War. This efficiency cannot be due exclusively to physical advantages and organization. It has been rendered possible partly by the necessity to unite or perish, and perhaps even more by the unity of purpose and the bonds of comradeship imbued into the different Soviet nationalities in spite of all the cruelties of the Revolution and of the present government.

However, the final test in the Russian minority policy has not yet come, though it is very near. It will lie in the capacity of Bolshevism to stick to its principle of toleration of diverse cultures in contact even with nationalities which can look back at an old national tradition of their own and are situated at the politically, culturally, and strategically exposed fron-

[12] *Ibid.* Appendix I, pp. 138. f.
[13] This and the following quotation is from Stalin's Political Report to the Sixteenth Congress of the Communist Party of the Soviet Union, July 1930. Taken from Hans Kohn, *op. cit.*, Appendix I, p. 153.

tiers of Russia. Such territories may be Finland, Poland, the
Balkan countries, and perhaps even Austria and Germany,
partly as new Russian acquisitions, partly as "spheres of influence." If the Soviet Union has the greatness and self-confidence to pursue a policy of political and economic unification together with a policy of cultural pluralism then it will
offer to desperate and downtrodden Europe a vision of a new
future. The spell of this vision may spread from France to
China and eventually help in building up the largest, most
self-sufficing, and at the same time culturally most productive
continent which ever existed in human history.

For the time being, however, it looks as if Bolshevik
political engineering were going to fall short of the idea of a
great multinational unity. On its western frontier Russia
seems to relapse into a form of territorial bargaining which
could not have been worse in the period of absolutist dynasticism. This may prove right to those observers who point at a
diminishing degree of cultural pluralism during the last
decade even within the older boundaries of the Soviet Union,
and who maintain that its nationality policy never issued
from a genuine cultural pluralism with an intrinsic appreciation for ethnic differences, but rather from a conception of a
class and party state for which differentiated national and
cultural sentiments are of inferior importance and can consequently be handled according to expediency. Perhaps it is
better to keep always in mind the preamble of the rules of
the Bolshevist party which says that the Soviet Union is "a
unified militant organization held together by conscious, iron
proletarian discipline." [14]

But whatever the policy of the Soviet Union may be, in
face of the total crisis of Western civilization from which all
the totalitarian systems have profited, the democratic countries can no longer permit themselves to recommend to the
suffering world beautiful liberal ideals on which alone it
cannot live. Democracy is now challenged to present to the
world not only a philosophy with its roots in a glorious past,

[14] Hula, *op. cit.*, p. 197.

but also a policy of action which leads toward the final liberation of all the indigenous forces latent in every nationality and minority. Only so can the strife of nations be changed into an order in which the heritage of individualism can be truly merged with the idea of social co-operation. What humanity needs, is a pluralistic social democracy of free nations.

B. Emergence of the Masses

Closely connected with the development of modern nationalism and all its conflicts is the change in the social position of the masses. This change also results from the growing self-assertion of the human individual since the period of the Renaissance. The positive part in the philosophy underlying both the rise of nationality and the rise of the masses is the Christian concept of human dignity and the categorical imperative that no human being should be used as an instrument for purposes alien to him, but be regarded as an end in himself. The negative side in both nationality and the modern movement of the masses lies in the fact that they tend to defeat their own original goal, the liberation of the individual, by confusing the means and the end. Thus the nation and the state become idols ready to devour the freedom of the citizen for whom they exist; and the mass, or the class, may destroy man's individuality instead of liberating it through co-operative action.

But modern mass and class struggle, like modern nationalism, also can be explained as a result of growing secularization. For the less men place their final hopes on a life beyond with reward for the pious and the poor and with punishment for the wicked, the more they will endeavor to fill their earthly existence with the possible maximum of happiness. Their concrete existence, not final unification with the Eternal, will be their first interest. Either they get their share as long as they live here on earth, or they have lost the game. It is in recognition of these attitudes that potentates and privileged classes have always shown an intense solicitude for the piety of their subjects, much more than for their own. And it is for the same reason that fighters for the liberation of the masses have characterized religion as "the opiate of the people."

But besides individualism and secularism there have been other stimuli to drive the masses out of lethargy. Some of them, republicanism or democracy, and public education, have been introduced by the bourgeois class, which during the nineteenth century was gradually forced to admit that the fundamental human claims in its liberal ideology transcended the interests of a special caste and demanded the application to humanity as a whole, including their own workers.

The thinker who clearly foresaw this development was Karl Marx. It is easy to point at the many errors in his theory. Yet, the fact remains that no other thinker ever influenced the course of history so much as he did. For on his analyses of the economic process and his theory of the struggle of classes as the driving force in social change is based Bolshevism, the rival of the capitalist-democratic societies.

The reference to Marx adds another explanation of modern mass movements to those of individualism and secularism; namely, the factor of collectivistic defense of those without, against those with capital. This process of a shifting of power from a relatively few to the masses and their representatives, or at least of division of power between capital and labor, is far from finished. In some countries it just begins. However, its various consequences are already strong enough to throw the world into convulsions that make us sometimes doubt whether the fever indicates the recovery or the death of the present culture.

No doubt, except during war, in most countries the external life of the worker has improved during the past eighty years, as a consequence of the rise of wages and better working conditions. After all, it could not be worse than it was in the decades of early and unchecked industrialism! Furthermore, in the democratic countries the worker has been admitted to the polls. Even in modern dictatorial countries the dictators have to appoint a host of propagandists; in order to spread the gospel they need pamphlets, mass meetings in beer halls, 'strength through joy' activities, processions, *panem et circenses,* and, if all this does not work, public trials. Generally, in modern totalitarian situations the party in power must present itself to the people as its true guardian; only for this reason can it dare claim the right to abolish all other parties and to be identified with the State and the Nation.

Therefore it is erroneous to compare modern dictatorships with the older absolutist monarchies. In the latter the king held his place "by the grace of the Lord," whereas the modern dictator is just "the leader"; to him the grace, or the *Charisma,* does not come from above, but from below— not from God, but from the masses and those who finance the enterprise. The leader's career is finished with his defeat by an enemy, whereas the monarch, even in modern times, may survive because his house is rooted in the past of the nation.

It is in recognition of this defect that modern totalitarianism uses all possible means for creating a mythical halo around its brief tradition. Bolshevism has the Tomb of Lenin, just as Islam has the Ka'ba, and Christianity the Holy Sepulchre. Italian Fascism played around with the old Roman fasces, and National Socialism needed symbols such as the swastika and the Third Reich to create the necessary glitter around its devilish humbuggery.

But in spite of all these advances of the once despised plebeians, or at least the sham concessions made to them, the success of the masses is incomplete even in democracies. Being without the concrete means of power, such as money, machines, and the command over the army, they have to rely on collectivistic representation, and they never know to whom they surrender their influence.

In addition, the modern masses have not really achieved what we could call a 'socialist culture.' No country has yet struck a balance between the demand for a civilization for all and a civilization which satisfies the individual's demand for standards to go with a full life.

One reason for this dilemma is that, ideologically, the emergence of the masses has often been connected with an unreal concept of equality. 'Equality' represents a rightful claim of man, in so far as it symbolizes the idea of the brotherhood of men and the right to see talent developed and appreciated, irrespective of birth, class, and race. On the other hand the concept of equality is doomed to disillusion and embarrass exactly its most ardent believers, if they understand by it something like a total and natural equality of men with respect to both their abilities and the rewards arising from them. The moment such a concept becomes dominant in a society, the claim of excellence, which we stated in our first chapter as one of the basic conditions of progress, is no longer listened to. Rather, together with the sense for a natural hierarchy of accomplishments true equality and human comradeship also go out, and the cult of incompetence, jealousy, and a plebeian delight in mediocrity enter into the vacuum.

Therefore democracy's concept of equality must be dynamic and recognize the value of difference. The recognition of the basic dignity of the human individual before God, man, and law must not exclude, but rather include interest in, and just reward of talent and effort. I am equal to my fellow man not only because I happen to exist, but much more because my specific contribution to society—like his—is justly valued according to its quality, social effect, and even with respect to its rarity, as far as rarity is not snobbishness, but conducive to the widening of the scale of human experience.

We live now in a period when we have to pay a heavy penalty for the merely egalitarian concept of equality in our social and cultural life.

For modern societies have failed to utilize the necessary "natural elite" of which Jefferson dreamed and which his period produced in men such as himself, Washington, Franklin, and John Adams. Modern societies tend either to create plutocracies, or political cliques of sometimes extremely dubious moral qualities. We have astoundingly little organic outlet for personal merit into the arteries of public life and, as a consequence, we have increasing difficulty in finding the right men for positions of importance.

Culturally, we produce more and more schools and colleges, more and more holders of doctorate titles, and fewer and fewer people who are appreciative of cultural values as the necessary protection of mankind against relapsing into barbarism. Nowhere has the truly cultured person a more difficult stand than among the truly half-educated, more and more of whom reach high up into the college world. Our production of books, magazines, and newspapers is enormous —and so is our cult of vulgarity.

But there is no inspiration in mediocrity, particularly as religion and other great spiritual motives of life have been drowned under the avalanche of modern demi-enlightenment. Dimly the masses realize that they are not on the right track. Politically they have become cynical about the big machinery of parties and about the functionaries who control them. They are afraid that the final power still rests in those who possess the instruments of production and the means to feed the octopus of propaganda. Most of all, in spite of all endeavors the masses have been incapable of combatting successfully the evils of war, insecurity, and unemployment. The old feudal overlords have been ousted in most countries—in some countries even the bourgeoisie—but other even more powerful forces have occupied the vacant thrones.

The situation becomes all the more difficult, as, in spite of the glorification of equality, there is also the glorification of mobility. Everybody endowed with push and energy, desires to rise above "the mass of the people." Thus vocations and social groups, which in earlier times created leaders of national and international fame out of their own ranks, become depleted of talent and must allow strangers, mostly professional lawyer-politicians to represent them. One of the saddest spectacles in the European countries between the two World Wars was the growing alienation of the working people from their more or less professional political representatives. This alienation offered a welcome target for all anti-democratic and anti-labor parties. United against their common enemy, namely social democracy, they brought about the end of all free workers' associations in the fascist countries. There were people even in France, England, and other countries who welcomed this manifestation of the weakness of organized labor. They hoped to become free of any control from below, unaware that they witnessed the first stage of the collapse of European humanism. For the emergence and organization of the masses has become a factor in modern history which, like nationalism, cannot be eradicated but must be properly directed. Any attempt at a violent solution is bound to create first some sort of fascism, then chaos. There has been transmitted to us a saying of Lycurgus: "The Gods do nothing until they have blinded the minds of the wicked." This seemingly holds true as long as the human race persists.

The emergence of modern mass movements is historically and sociologically inseparable from the growth of the modern city.

Through the city the new industrial society offers the masses many more opportunities than the older agricultural society—otherwise there would not be the constant flight from the country into "the centers of modern life." City life provides a certain degree of chance and mobility (though in a constantly decreasing ratio); it offers intellectual satisfaction to the curious and a lot of distractions and freedom from restricting customs and mores; furthermore, in spite of many deprivations, there is more leisure and comfort in a small city apartment than in a small farm where the two cows, the horse, and the chickens must be taken care of continuously. Things would not have gone as they did had the whole development been totally averse to Human Nature.

But Human Nature is an unreliable lady. She may lure us into short pleasures at the expense of more enduring happiness, and mere rapidity in the succession of stimuli may feed on the wealth and peace of our souls. In a way, the modern city dweller leads a life of superficiality in a completely man-made world. The great powers of the universe no longer speak to him through nature; loyalties, in the best case, reach only from person to person, but not from persons to abiding and emotionally laden objects like the father's farm and the hills and fields around it. Most experiences become measured merely in terms of money or pleasure; the blessings of enduring love for things, however simple, are stolen away by the hustle of the daily business and innumerable little enticements. Often even these enticements do not exist, and there remains nothing but the daily routine of mechanical work, the long walks to and from the factory, a dull family life, and perhaps unemployment.

Under such conditions, positive and negative together, knowledge, desires, and excitability grow, while stability and human substance are constantly jeopardized. But this is exactly the situation under which man is most exposed to all the negative characteristics of mass psychology: fear of solitude and desire to surrender oneself and his reasoning to the crowd, dependence on influences from outside instead of ripening of beliefs and attitudes from within, and the replacement of deeply moored values by easily changing and mainly material desires.

All these factors together necessarily engender a society completely different from the older society of farmers and craftsmen who formed the bulk of the fighters in the American Revolution.

This revolution is still today an interesting subject for the study of mass movements because it succeeded in avoiding the danger of uncontrollable and illusory radicalism which so easily grows out of the very dynamic of revolutionary action.

For the American Revolution was not a result of an internal social crisis, but an act of political self-assertion of a growing and healthy society against a foreign power with its center on the other side of the Atlantic; perhaps the whole enterprise should not be called a "revolution," but a war of liberation. The second reason for the success of the American venture in liberty lies with the realism of the leaders of the Revolution. This realism has been criticized by historians as a lack of principles; it was, in fact, a mixture of practical idealism, shrewdness, egotism, and insight into the limits of the possible, and thus one of the most perfect examples of political wisdom.

But that wisdom could exert itself only because the leaders could count on followers who, rough, business-minded, and often uneducated though they were, were nevertheless not parts of a "mass" in the modern sociological and mainly negative sense of the word. In contrast to the French, the American revolutionary idealism was anchored in a realistic appreciation of the factors and forces of social life, and therefore was successful. The French revolutionary idealism was overnourished with the vitamins of Rousseauism, and had to flatter the proletariat of the city of Paris; therefore it failed.

But in comparison to the modern masses, say of New York and Chicago, those of Paris around 1790 were still living a somewhat organic life. In all his poverty, certainly greater than that of the workingmen in our modern world centers, the little *citoyen de Paris* was still in contact with guilds, corporations, groups of neighbors, and ideas, which gave him more personal hold than the mixture of mass life and loneliness to which so many modern American city dwellers are exposed, particularly if they come from foreign countries and races.

If, through a combination of circumstances which are not at all beyond human imagination, these men are driven into revolutionary actions, they will by far surpass in violence their revolutionary ancestry of past centuries.

C. *The Claims of Labor*

Albeit, our concern with the problem of the masses stems not from fear of riot and revolution but from a respect for the human rights of the industrial population which claims its share in the benefits of civilization. Either we will have a civilization fully participated in by the total population as far as it is capable of profiting thereby, or we will have no civilization.

But how can we approximate this goal?

One of the hopeful signs of a gradually increasing contact between modern culture and the working population is the growing appreciation of the value of manual labor.

We know from ancient sources that manual labor, except agriculture, was in low repute. It is difficult to say whether Plato in his *Republic* looks down to the "iron class," which represents for him the craftsmen and farmers, or whether with his distinction of this group from the "golden class" of the philosopher-guardians and the "silver class" of the soldiers he wishes to indicate primarily a sociological fact. However, in Aristotle, as well as in other ancient writers, there are enough statements in which manual work is relegated to the slaves or to classes not far away from them. The craftsman who works for pay carries with him the mark of inferiority.

Much of this ancient prejudice was accepted by the cultural leaders of the Middle Ages. They misinterpreted Aristotle's appreciation of the "contemplative life" in a sense that made it superior to the active life, and the farther away the active life was from the contemplative, the more they held it removed from the true mission of man. However, the Christian concept of man, the absence of slavery as Antiquity had it and the role of the guilds of craftsmen in the medieval city, all this bespeaks a much greater appreciation of manual labor in the times of Thomas Aquinas than in the times of Aristotle.

Still more in our times we consider it good style to profess our belief in the dignity and the rights of labor. This distinguishes us from certain "aristocrats" of older times as well as from the charitably minded people of the first half of the nineteenth century who discussed the foundation of schools for the children of workers primarily under the motto: "Open a school and close a jail." If today most parents of the more favored classes wish their children to choose other than manual work, it is not because they despise it—although some continue to give it a social stigma—but because it is more uncomfortable, more insecure, often less profitable (though decreasingly so), and for these accompanying qualities less esteemed than white-collar vocations.

Nevertheless, there is some improvement, and this is the result of two factors.

The first is modern technology. In contrast to Aristotle we have learned to respect applied thinking, the kind which has created the modern machine, the modern plant, and their thousandfold products. There is a decisive change in the interests of the most intelligent parts of youth. Up to the end of the nineteenth century the majority preferred humanistic studies and professions built on these; after that the interests swung over toward the sciences and their different applications. There is an enormous possibility for physical and intellectual adventures in the exploration of nature and in engineering; modern nations feel that their survival depends to a large degree on the efficiency of laboratories and of industrial devices; some even believe that this is the only factor that counts in civilization.

There is also a romantic element in the noise of a modern steel plant and in the heat and color of melting iron; a whole literature has arisen which describes the gamut of human sentiments from horror to admiration in the face of modern industry. Furthermore, in the United States the salary of many elementary-school teachers is far below that of a skilled worker, at least in times of boom. If the endeavors to regulate wages and working hours, and to provide security and dignified leisure succeed, then the gap between the workmen and the white-collar people will continually decrease. Let us hope not through the lowering of the life standard of the second, but through the rise of the first group.

The other factor which has brought about a higher esteem of labor is progressive education. It has brought home to parents the educational value of manual work and it has taught children the delight as well as the difficulties which lie in craft. Furthermore, in co-operation with modern industrial artists, the progressive teacher has shown the potential artistic element inherent even in modern mass production. Theoretically, the recognition of the educational value of craft is not new; the educators of the Renaissance spoke about it and the great Swiss educator Pestalozzi considered training of the hand as necessary for the maturation of a full personality as training of the brain and the heart.

But we must guard against false optimism. For to the same degree that modern technology has increased our respect for mechanical production, so has it created the gigantic mass of modern unskilled laborers. The relation of skilled to unskilled workers in the United States is about one to two, specifically 6,282,687 to 14,012,869 in 1930. In between the two is the floating mass of semi-skilled workers (7,977,-572). Sociologists, psychologists, and educators try to mitigate the mental consequences of unskilled labor by devices in the timing and rhythm of the work and by creating emotional attachments to it; many books have been written about the use of leisure and the opportunities of adult education to induce human values into the life of the mechanical worker.

Yet, there are obstacles hard to overcome. The main difficulty lies in the structure of the human mind itself. Compelled to devote eight hours of the day to merely mechanical tricks which nevertheless need concentration, human beings cannot easily switch over to creative forms of leisure and read good books understandingly, or listen to good music, or whatever else well-intended social reformers recommend.

One must also take into account that—with exceptions, of course—those parts of the population tend to fill the ranks of unskilled labor who have not had the chance, or the talent, to develop genuine interest in intellectual or esthetic activities. The remedy in this respect is not in trying by hook or by crook to transfer forms of mental recreations adequate for the intellectually active people over into the army of the intellectually passive. The ordinary mind cannot suddenly change from familiar routine work into unaccustomed and consequently difficult forms of mental activity. Rather we have to create dignified forms of leisure which are fitted for the specific psychological situation of the mechanical worker. They are to be found wherever human energy can be enjoyably released through recreational physical work which appeals to the total person and contains, in addition to the factor of enjoyment an opportunity for some kind of thinking and emotional satisfaction. Such forms of leisure are gardening, hiking, and other ways of living with nature. There is sport, especially of the uncompetitive sort; and for those who are artistically talented—there are amazingly many among unskilled workers—there exist great possibilities of development in painting and modeling courses, and in choirs and orchestras, for good and simple music can be played with simple instruments after relatively little training.

The values which lie in more intellectual and verbal forms of adult education, or in the radio, should not be denied, but for the large majority of unskilled workers concrete and somewhat physical forms of recreation will be more constructive. They will also contribute more to citizenship education than most of us, caught in a primarily intellectual concept of education, are inclined to believe. No doubt, good citizenship needs a good deal of brains, but for those whose strength is not in their brains common activities connected with nature, the exercise of the human body, and the right emotional satisfaction will create more inner harmony and a better sense for what is wholesome or not, than any kind of verbal discussion and superficial enlightenment can do. Certainly such seemingly simple recreations as here indicated can also help create small cells of community life in which a genuine feeling for democratic and joyful living may arise.

But all this necessitates moving the industrial worker out of the unhealthy and congested areas of our big cities, which in turn is impossible without the decentralization of industrial production. Modern technology has proved that such decentralization is not only possible but could be even more productive than our big plants, provided long-range planning is applied.[15] Thus one of the most powerful motives, powerful particularly in a competitive society; namely profit, would no longer require all the ugliness and unhealthiness in which a large part of adults and their children are forced to live.

The time has come when modern politics, both national and local, must recognize the intimate relation of industrial planning to the creation and preservation of democratic citizenship among the masses. The conditions of civilization of which we spoke at the beginning of this book cannot be produced in overcrowded cities, even if there is sufficient bread and work. For enjoying his life under the strain of modern industrial production, for gaining the strength of faith and hope even in a simple form of life, and for sharing personal and civic responsibilities with his fellow men, man needs not so much radios and movies as a walk in fresh air, and a piece of garden, and a neighbor whom he meets in leisure, not only at the work bench and on the staircase of a tenement house.

In view of these facts it is most unfortunate that the need for accelerated production during this war has compelled American industry to prefer short-range to long-range planning and to crowd industrial workers in rapidly organized centers. Thus families have been herded together having nothing in common but the necessity of earning their living at the same place. Children without care from father and mother try to escape the anxiety of lonely and loveless life by running to the streets where the girls in as early an age as thirteen and fourteen become exposed to prostitution and venereal diseases. Rather than speaking about the worth of

[15] See works of Lewis Mumford on this subject.

the human soul which—as is true in certain cases—is stronger
than its environment, it is more democratic to say that conditions like these are bound to create rabble and criminals,
instead of a democratic community. Community life needs a
feeling of mutual responsibility, of a tradition which can
incorporate newcomers, and, in addition to the daily work
and drudgery, some common purpose, pleasure, and recreation.

Without such values local politics becomes a racket; if the
communities fail to produce the sound substratum and the
first concrete school of national self-administration, how can
we administer a whole country and preserve a free society?
A part of politics is the formation of groups with homogene-
ous interests, which—unfortunately—involves the exclusion
of other groups with deviating interests. But if these striving
parties within a nation have nothing at all in common, if
there is, in spite of all struggle, no mutual understanding
and sense of common directives, then democracy will be
wrecked. For then parties transform themselves either into
fortified camps with no suggestion from the other side being admitted, or into fleeting conglomerations of interest, or
even into gangs ready for rioting and shooting. In the early
frontier towns of the West, which were as yet only settle-
ments, one of the most desired articles, and that one most
advertised in sales catalogues, was a revolver, because very
often cartridges decided conflicts which in more settled communities would have been decided by representatives of the
differing parties appearing before a common tribunal.

When after the defeat of Germany in the first World War
the so-called revolution of 1918 broke out, workers who had
been accustomed to organized community life and labor
unions behaved in an exemplary way; this to such a degree
that the elimination of reactionary powers, which justifies
the perils of revolutions, was not carried through. On the
other hand in such towns which, in consequence of rapidly
established industries, were nothing but uncomfortable dwell-
ing places of not yet communized crowds, riots were frequent

for which the term revolution is much too honorific. It was not a clash between organized groups with political ideas and responsible leaders, but of uprooted and nervous crowds seeking an outlet for their feelings of bitterness and despair. The origin of modern fascism has many psychological similarities with these events of 1918, and the success of all modern revolutions has been imperiled by nothing so much as by the rabble which did not understand their deeper meaning.

But it is, in the long run, futile to imagine that a mass can be altered into an active and democratic group primarily by methods working upon it from outside. The essence of every educational process lies in the transformation of passiveness into energy; this applies to communities as well as to whole groups.

In this failure to create spontaneous energy lies the danger of all centralized action from above—from the mechanical system of doles and relief for the unemployed as exercised by unimaginative societies during the past decades of economic crisis, up to the governmental support or regulation of big industries which are in danger of losing their market. Continual search for help from outside changes a society of enterprise into a society of receivers, and when there is no more to receive, it becomes anarchical or cries for a dictator. If there is still any possibility for the salvation or, better, the creation of a social *and* democratic civilization, then it can only be one with a dynamic corporative life which gives all of its capable members a sense of purpose and of activity.

In contrast to that the political participation of the average citizen in our present democratic system is rather mechanical. From adolescence he grows over into a full-fledged citizen without noticing it. Who would think in these days of the initiation rites which in earlier societies accompanied the transition from youth into manhood and public responsibilities? Of course, there are the young men who have fought for their country and in this way received the supreme baptism of sacrifice. But war and its excitement are so utterly different from civil life that the transfer from one kind of experience to the other is difficult, and for most people impossible. The two tracks do not touch each other. The veteran —unless he turns into the professional bragging hero— speaks rarely of battles because they remain a foreign and eerie element in his life when he shifts bravely over from war to the daily quiet work of peace. He does what most of his neighbors do; read the local newspaper, go to the polls, and criticize the government.

Yet, it is the *conditio sine qua non* of modern democracy that we change citizenship from a mere legal right into a proud responsibility. As such it was felt during the rise of modern parliamentarianism and is still alive in the smaller democracies such as Switzerland and the Scandinavian countries where the delegate and his constituency are related to each other in a kind of fellowship.

In large countries parliament and government have become an increasingly abstract affair dealing with highly technical problems of national and international scope. With respect to the remoteness of the parliament of large countries the Swiss, Jean Jacques Rousseau, stated already in the eighteenth century that the English people exercise their right of citizenship only once, while they vote, and after that they disappear into darkness. But as in so many cases, also here Rousseau was strong in criticism but weak in constructive proposal.

For some kind of delegation of power is inevitable in a large society with division of labor. But if this delegation changes into political indifference or even complete surrender, then it always indicates failure in meeting a deep social challenge. Every community either decays or keeps fertile the soil of human relationships which must nourish the more abstract levels of modern political life. In other words, there must be behind the central political representation a vital corporative life, and a society which feels its unity in spite of all its divergencies. The social significance of smaller communities, of associations of employers, of physicians, lawyers, scholars, and of workers lies not only in their pursuing justified group interests. It also lies in their being potential cells of contact, first among people belonging to the specific ingroup, then between the ingroup and outer groups. They can motivate exchange of ideas and common action among men and women, and thus form the centers of the continual mutual education of adults without which no modern society can exist.

The foreigner is often astonished at the amount of committee work which goes on in this country. Even Americans are sometimes cynical about it, and rightly so, if they see the waste of time in meetings which after much discussion about a most obvious need decide to make an expensive survey and thus bury action in reports destined to disappear in the well-ordered files of foundations and libraries. European nations with an exaggerated examination system used to ridicule themselves by saying that their population consisted of two halves, one of them always busy in examining the other. The United States, a satirical person could say, has become the country in which one part of the population sits in committees and writes reports which the other part never bothers to read.

Yet, in the long run the educative effect which flows from all these meetings of smaller groups back into the total nation, is probably far more effective than the directives of bureaucrats and the streamlined efficiency of expert agencies which, from the point of immediate efficiency, could take care of many public concerns in a much briefer time than the many committees.

It is one of the many great blessings extended by fate to the English nation that at a time when the conditions of the working classes were the most miserable in the whole history of the country the many religious sects and conventicles gave the poor man a feeling of belonging to a group of equals in which he could maintain his feeling of dignity through common converse with his fellows in an atmosphere of reverence. In contrast, the poor people of the Continent were largely deprived of such a possibility of association and, at the same time, of individuality. The many social effects of this difference in the life of the masses can still be observed in the history of the European nations. Despite all hardship the English worker has remained in the tradition of his nation, though in terms of education he received much less from it than a worker's child received in Germany.

In the building up of a spirit of organic belongingness—which is the only means to avoid the degeneration of a group into a mass—modern trade-unionism will have to play a role of which many of its leaders seem not yet to be aware. Will trade-unionism be merely an agency for the representation of wage interests and other concerns of the workers, however important, or will it, by direct or indirect means, attempt to provide at least part of the experiences of full and expanding living of which modern industry has deprived them?

If the workers' unions do not make this attempt, then, against their own intention, they will be incapable of preventing the large masses from sliding into some kind of mechanical collectivism, in which the voluntary solidarity of free men will gradually be extinguished by some kind of extraneous control, whether fascist or bolshevist in character.

For let us remember again and again that the criterion of the social effectiveness of associations lies not only in what they do for themselves, but also in what they do and attempt to do for the whole community. Only such an attitude makes them ready for new actions and ideas and saves them from the narrowing and isolating effect of group egotism.

It was the very system of guilds and corporations which in its good times gave medieval man the security of mutual assistance, the pride of social esteem, responsibility for his community in times of peace and war, and in religious processions. When at the end of the Middle Ages corporative life decayed, the bright and manifold colors of medieval feudalism shaded over into absolutist regimentation from above.

Thus, in the last analysis, the modern problem of the emergence of the masses turns out to be educational. Only education, conceived of as an opportunity for ever widening experience and responsibility for themselves and others, can save people from the dullness under which they surrender to anything which promises incorporation, security, and thrill. The motto which workers' movements throughout the world took over from Francis Bacon, namely, that knowledge is power, is false and true at the same time. It is false if by knowledge, or by education, is meant nothing but "useful instruction." This alone leads toward technology which, in the long run, may destroy rather than build up civilization. The right kind of education is not only informative, but guarantees a relation of all people to common sources of inspiration. Only under such conditions can the individual pursue his daily work according to properly understood self-interest and, at the same time, perceive his roots in the common cultural ground of his nation and of humanity, and live accordingly.

III. CONCLUDING REMARKS

A. *The Main Bearers of Responsibility*

The great problems and issues of politics discussed in the previous sections present an enormous challenge particularly to three great nations which, for years to come, will have to decide not only about their own future, but will condition that of other nations.

These three will be England together with its dominions, the Soviet Republics, and the United States of America. The form in which they discharge their responsibility will be their trial before the court of history and the ultimate justification for their victory.

In one way the accumulation of power in a few nations, as we experience it now, is frightening. On the other hand, it is also a promise. For the change from jealous and aggressive into constructive power can occur only when the fear complex disappears which has driven peoples into a continual hysteria of self-assertion. Only really great power, both physical and mental, can afford to be fearless.

For achieving the superior wisdom we demand, the nations will have to develop, in theory as well as in practice, a science of politics which is conscious of the basic conditions of human civilization expounded in this book. So far, the ignorance of statesmen and of their nations about the fundamentals of effective social guidance has been appalling, so appalling that one may wonder whether nations and their leaders have preferred not to see truth—like sick persons who obstruct their own recovery because they do not wish to abandon old habits.

One can often read that the present political crisis is primarily a "moral" crisis and that, consequently, the world must first be improved morally before things can become better. Certainly with more actual consciousness of the dignity of man we would not have slid into the present catastrophe. But where does the moral crisis come from? Moral standards are not their own source. Their development—at least in part—is in proportion to the mastery of man over the difficulties in his natural and social environments.

Modern man is in such a miserable situation not because he likes war and immorality more than his ancestors, but because his mastery over the social environment, or his "social methodology," lags so immensely behind his mastery over nature, his "mechanical methodology," or "technology."

Either future generations will succeed in growing out of a timid prescientific attitude with respect to social problems and dare develop politics from the present state of alchemy and obscurantism into a systematic enterprise, both theoretical and applied, or we all will become slaves under a powerfully advancing industrial technology. Not well-intended social missionaries, nor typical party leaders, nor amateur diplomats and political lawyers can solve the problems. Practical experience and systematic scholarship of all branches, natural and humanistic, must work together.

Without contradicting our demand for a new scientific approach to politics, we could also say that the ultimate responsibility of the great bearers of power is inspirational in nature. It has to provide both practical and spiritual ways through which peoples can find security, purpose, and the right release for their energies.

Continual discussion of political philosophies, necessary though it may be, often achieves nothing more than to make people too conscious and fearful of discrepancies; only agreement about common action can bring about some kind of co-operation between such different systems as democracy and bolshevism. With increased sharing in action, the differences which in theory appear insurmountable may become more and more academic.

However the purposes for political action must be sought not merely in the international area. They ought, first of all, to be seen where they await our attention most impatiently, namely at home. Any attempt at improving the life of other peoples which is not rooted in similar interests and actions at home is escape. It is the same escape we find in individuals who are constantly occupied with other people's troubles because they do not dare see themselves realistically. On the other hand, concerns rooted and settled at home transcend narrow boundaries and carry with them an urge for universal action. Hence, though we recommend that people begin at home we do not recommend that they stop at home; rather we mean that right and sympathetic initiative can come only from men and nations whose own moral substance is sufficiently strong and virulent.

If each of the great nations were really interested in helping all its citizens at home toward a life as full and expanding as possible, then it would also increasingly realize that its own welfare depends on the welfare of the other nations.

This is true not only in a material sense. It is still more the case with respect to the cultural conditions of civilization, for no nation can constantly replenish its intellectual and spiritual resources out of its own energy. If it does so it will soon be exhausted. The Anglo-Saxon democracies, for example, will always need the European continent to avoid cultural inbreeding. Even for their economic development they will have to watch without prejudice the experiments of other countries. Russia will not fully develop unless it dares expose itself to the world outside. In all Western nations metaphysical thought has reached the point of desiccation and needs enrichment from the religious reservoirs of Asia, as it did at the end of Antiquity. Science becomes increasingly international. Finally, how can the devastated nations of the European continent, which once were the cradle of Western culture, restore themselves unless they learn to co-operate with other peoples? Either Europe becomes again rich in contacts with all the other nations and continents, or it will become culturally and politically the same as it is geographically, an appendage to Asia.

But the development of bold new forms of politics needs, first of all, co-operation among the great powers.

Should a catastrophe occur and the unity of the three major nations break into pieces, then the chances for Russia obviously, are very propitious. Russia has a coherent and at the same time extremely elastic political philosophy and derives from it a similar policy of action. The Anglo-Saxon countries, in the meantime, are passing through a transition from the nineteenth-century capitalistic concept of democracy toward a social democracy whose structure cannot yet be clearly defined.

Russia, with the unforseeable possibilities of its neighborhood to great Asiatic territories, will develop on a geographically united territory without a colonial system. Race prejudices, the curse of the white race, seem to play a minor role in the Soviet Republics. The English Empire on the other hand will always be in extreme jeopardy because of its difficult life-lines through which it may again be involved in highly perilous situations.

In all likelihood, bolshevism would not appeal to the majority of the population of Western Europe if they lived under normal conditions. They will not so easily forget the cruelty of the Bolshevist revolution, the "purges," and the lack of democratic rights, all characteristics which bring communism and fascism very close together.

Against this the believers in the future of bolshevism can say that Russia never went through a liberal period, that the tyranny of the Communist party was not worse than that of the older Czarist system and that, in contrast to the older monarchy, bolshevism has raised the cultural level of the people. They may also point at the many social defects within the democracies themselves.

With respect to the countries of the European continent west of Russia, they may state that their populations have tested all the different forms of monarchy, democracy, and fascism and seen them failing; that they have been humiliated and debased by their own governments and lived for several winters in bombed houses, eaten from the community kitchen, and seen their families destroyed partly by war and partly by the secret police. Why, after all these experiences, might they not find hope in some sort of collectivism? If not for themselves, then for their children. A new western European collectivism need not be a slavish imitation of Russian Marxism. It may be that some of the smaller western nations develop first within their own boundaries, and then co-operatively, economic and political systems which guarantee unity and security together with pluralism and variety. In history, ruins have been not only eternal documents of devastation; they have also served as the foundation for new and courageous structures.

B. *Summary*

Politics, in its noble and fundamental sense, is the application of our insight into the social trends and forces which come from the past, are present, and will be in the future. We can master these trends and forces only if we understand them;

they will become destructive if, in consequence of inertia or evil intention, we try to ignore or escape their operations.

Hence those who are responsible for our political future—in a way, everybody is—have to face courageously the main issues with which we are confronted as political citizens of our nation and the world.

First, we must pull ourselves out of the fallacious contrast of individualism or liberalism on the one, and collectivism on the other hand. In a sound nation the two are not hostile to each other, but interact in a manner to secure the fullest development of the individual through the help of his society, and the fullest development of society through the help of individuals.

If understood in our sense, politics becomes one of the great organized ethical enterprises of mankind. For it can secure the mutual give and take between the part and the whole only if it feels its responsibility for providing the physical and spiritual conditions under which men can live a secure and dignified life. But there is also the inevitable conflict between politics and ethics as a consequence of the intimate connection of politics with power. Whereas normal civic intercourse has progressed sufficiently to replace physical force by legality, political life is permeated with all kinds of competition more mighty than all law and legality. Especially international life has remained in a more or less barbaric state. We all suffer from this and search desperately for salvation, but we have not yet found the organization strong enough to secure peace among mankind. This is partly due to external physical forces stronger than our will and intelligence. But the reason why these forces are beyond our power lies in the fact that we have not yet discovered valid logical and ethical principles for decision in times of international danger. Should we overcome the barbaric state of strife among nations by strict declaration of nonviolence or pacifism, or should we accept the challenge of power and attempt to combine with it wisdom and planning in order to increasingly substitute co-operation for force?

We may admire nonviolence or pacifism, provided it is not a mere rationalization of escape from hard responsibilities. But most men feel that the insistence on this attitude in a world as yet unwilling to apply it universally may encourage the aggressor and eventually unite the world not in peace and freedom, but under dictatorial powers.

However, those who in view of this possibility decide to meet power on its own battlefields, must avoid priding themselves as the brave "realists" in contrast to the "dreamers" in the camps of the pacifists or other followers of the gospel of Christ. For there are two levels of realism, one which looks at, and decides in relation to, the immediate problems and postpones the question as to what will come afterwards. But another, and perhaps the deeper level of realism, dares set the great and permanent commands of constructive human life—nonviolence, peace, truth, and love—against the expediencies and compromises of the day. There are many who think that for the very preservation of these values war may be necessary; the pacifist, however, can point to the fact that most frequently in history the victory of one fighting power over the other never resulted in the elimination of evils; only the executor changed. Mostly the victorious power took over the heritage of injustice from its enemy, and suffered in its soul more than it won by the booty of its victory.

As things stand now the heroic declaration of nonviolence even by small groups is of importance, for it renders visible the demand of human conscience in a world of crime; thus it serves as a challenge to nations which, in spite of all their sins against their own professed ethics, acknowledge the moral heritage of humanity as an inner obligation.

The greatest hindrance to international co-operation has been the intensive emphasis on nationality which in the Christian Western world began in the times of the Renaissance and has steadily increased since then. However, it would be erroneous to see in modern nationalism nothing but a sinister power. Rather we must understand it as the extension of feelings of individualism from the person to the

group to which he belongs, or as an act of identification of
the independent citizen with the nation in which he sees the
framework and shelter of his own personal development and
culture.

That is to say, nationality, just as modern individualism,
cannot be fought by means of suppression, in spite of all its
actual and potential perils. Attempts at extirpation only lead
to frustration and aggressive forms of reaction. Nationality
must be acknowledged as a fundamental factor in modern
history, but it must be incorporated into a synthetic form of
international organization.

This form of organization is offered by the principle of
dual sovereignty which says that any national or ethnic group
that feels itself endowed with a specific cultural heritage
must be given the right to insist on the free development of
those values which the individual himself would consider an
essential part of his personal culture. To these values belong
particularly language, religion, education, and certain national mores which give to the life of a people its particular
charm and flavor. For lack of a better term we called these
values the *interna* of national life, and these *interna* should
be administered under full sovereignty of the specific nation, provided they are not harmful to the common interests
of mankind.

On the other hand the principle of dual sovereignty says
that all these political and economic interests of a nation
should be co-ordinated with the interests of other nations
which are technical means for the achievement of practical
aims. These mediate values, or *externa* of national life, are,
by definition, not ends in themselves. They are in the service
of the greatest welfare of the majority of a people and of
humankind. While our language, our religion, and our moral
convictions cannot be altered according to merely pragmatical considerations, we ought to accustom ourselves to the fact
that there is nothing holy in merely political or economic
sovereignty as such which forbids our subordinating it to the
exigencies of international peace and co-operation.

Only if in the future organization of the world we succeed in pursuing the principle of dual sovereignty instead of the principle of absolute sovereignty will we find the right hierarchy of social values which allows us to say what comes first and what comes next, what is an end and what is a means, and where the sacred dignity of man is at stake or merely his egotistic interests. Thus we may be able to construct a world where variety of cultures can be harmonized with unity in political action.

If we fail to go this way a great number of absolute states, big and small, will live beside each other in an atmosphere of suspicion; minorities and smaller nations, in spite of all their possible contributions to human culture, will be in constant jeopardy, and finally the welfare and creativeness of mankind will be sacrificed for the continual preparation and the expenses of warfare.

Another historical outgrowth of modern individualism is the emerging self-consciousness of the masses. They refuse to be treated merely as instruments of society but wish to participate in the determination of their own future, of the future of their nations, and of the future of international policy. In the light of the common root of both nationality and mass self-assertion in individualism it may appear paradoxical that the two have often fought each other. Especially have the different labor internationals of the European continent developed political ideologies very contrary to those of nationality. The reason for this contrast is that the earlier labor internationals found the idea of nationality, just as the idea of liberalism, represented by power groups of feudal and bourgeois character which ruled the state for their own interests but not for those of the people and least of all for those of the working class. Thus the proletarian idea of "class struggle" worked against the idea of nationality which by necessity insisted on national unity.

The leading classes answered the dangers "from below" by decrying the workers as "unpatriotic fellows," though in every war they were invited to die in the trenches, and did

so. Unfortunately the slogan of defending the sacred trust of
patriotism against the "red internationalism" of the workers
was taken up also by the lower middle classes. The latter
were helplessly caught between the Scylla of big business and
the Charybdis of labor organizations and co-operatives. Nowhere perhaps could one find more political disorientation
and obstinacy to realistic political thinking than among the
small shopkeepers and artisans who fight desperately for
their economic and social independence. Yet, in their fear of
"sinking down in the proletariat" the lower middle classes
have generally listened willingly to the propaganda of the
nationalist "upper classes." They have tried to live up to
them at least ideologically, and did not discover that thus
they allowed themselves to be led by the nose. In almost
every country this unfortunate group has joined the reaction-
aries and fascists in their fight against labor.

In reality and in contrast to all denunciations, even against
all the international theories of labor leaders and Marxists,
the working masses have always rallied to the defense of
their countries. Sometimes, especially in 1914, one could
even have wished for a more enlightened distinction of the
socialist parties between patriotism and imperialism. But in
World War II it was mainly leftists who in the Nazi occupied countries led the underground movements. German
workers have fought the tyranny of Hitler more than any
other group, certainly more than the Protestant or the Catholic clergy, many of whom needed apparently a considerable
amount of experience before they discovered the true nature
of fascist totalitarianism. And the Russian workers have defeated Hitler's troops on the battlefield.

So the working classes in the European countries will no
longer be satisfied with some reforms in public education and
labor legislation, and otherwise withdraw—as after 1918—
into relative insignificance. They have proved too conspicu-
ously their willingness to bring patriotic sacrifices; in addition, they are too important in the productive process. In the
era of the bourgeoisie from the seventeenth to the nine-

teenth centuries the upper middle classes invaded the domain of power so far restricted to the nobility. Today we are in the period when the working class tries to share the influence of the older groups or, if excluded, may resort to revolutionary tactics as it has already done successfully in Russia. In so far as this general historical process of the shifting of classes is at stake, Marx' analysis of the importance of class struggle in the evolution of society has been correct. But as we have seen, he has erred in one extremely important aspect: the ascension of the working class has not come through the internationalism of the workers; it has come through their national heroism. This, however, may be but the first phase in a development; according to bolshevist dialectics the working classes will take up their international ideals after the problem of nationality has been solved from within each national group.

Consequently the future of Europe, and perhaps the future of civilization generally, will largely depend on a constructive interaction between the justifiable trends in nationalism and the justifiable claims of the working masses. They demand, as the first step, their place beside the other powers within the different nations—in so far they are national—and may then demand, as the second step, the unification of the world for the creation of general human welfare. This, of course, requires that they do not share the fate of the liberal movements (which also carried initially the double banner of nationality *and* internationality) and get stuck within merely national sentiments and egotisms. In addition, democracy will survive only in those countries in which the rising national and international influence of the working class will be fitted into a pattern of social humanism. For only in such an atmosphere can all the various individuals and groups make their specific contributions to the whole and at the same time profit from it. In countries where these conditions are not given, the future will lead toward some form of dictatorship, with a one party rule within the country, and nationalistic attitudes toward the outside.

Should this occur, then the world would eventually divide itself into several big industrialized territories of totalitarian character. For no country could then afford even the gesture of free international exchange of goods and ideas, but would seal itself hermetically within its own boundaries. For internal and external fighting the big powers would be armed to the teeth, and in comparison to their warfare the present forms of social struggle, and even the second World War, would be but preparations for the final Armageddon between classes and classes, and nations and nations.

We have only one choice. Either we are headed first toward a period when big and totalized industrial territories are engaged in wars of elimination and when, in addition, civil wars between bourgeoisie and industrial workers may shake the individual countries from within, or we must find forms of political and social organization that satisfy and, at the same time, combine the two gigantic trends of modern history, namely the trend toward nationality and the trend toward political self-assertion of the masses. That means, we must give the individual the opportunity to identify his own feeling of dignity with that of his country. But in order to play his role successfully within the nation and mankind he needs to be incorporated in a specific social group which he feels to be respected and in which he fulfills his specific and immediate vocation.

Only in this combination of direct corporate experiences at home, in the family, the community, the professional association or the union, with the more universal experiences of the citizen of the nation and of humanity can man be at home both in himself and the world, and make it a home for others.

Needless to say this combination of intimate corporate feelings with more general political aspirations is important not only with respect to the working class; employers and professionals need it just as much, and in spite of their better possibilities, they often have little of it. When, in this context, we are speaking primarily of the working class, it is in view of the fact that the enormous increase of the industrial population will change the politics of the future. This change will be catastrophic if the harmonization of this group with the best in our political and cultural tradition does not succeed; but in case of success it may offer completely new perspectives for the development of mankind.

There are hopeful signs of gradual incorporation of the large working masses into the framework of our national and international culture in the growing appreciation of manual labor. However, we must not overestimate this factor, for it can be merely emotional without practical consequences. For the stability of our society—in addition to the rejuvenation of corporate life—much has to be done in terms of modern industrial reorganization and city planning, for only under a conducive physical environment can constructive social attitudes develop.

But we must give up the notion, which in its essence is a hangover from old absolutism and patriarchalism, that there can be a socially effective policy which thinks and plans merely *for* the masses. Rather the masses must make their own effort. Understood in this sense, the effect of all future social policy will depend upon the degree to which the people in each nation, and eventually in all nations, will take up their own social and cultural education as one of their noblest duties. Here lies the enormous significance of future adult education, which is not yet understood in all its historical responsibilities and consequences.

In these concluding remarks we have reviewed the great political problems the solution of which will decide the future of our civilization. Every man and every nation will share in responsibility. With respect to the cultural development of mankind the smaller nations may have to contribute even more than the great powers because the natural self-interest of minorities generally conforms with peace and culture. Yet, there are some gigantic political problems in respect to which the big victorious nations of the second World War will have to act as trustees of all humanity. Either they make it possible to build up a new world or they will destroy everything. If they have nothing else to offer but a big power policy of the prewar type—which was a mixture of pomposity, helplessness, and timidity—then the consequence will be first a new system of entangling alliances, and then new wars. The people all over the world must ask from the governments of the great powers action based on a scientific and ethical insight into the nature of the social problems which they will meet in ever varying forms: the problems of individualism and collectivism, of the right or wrong use of power, of nationalities and minorities, and of capital and labor.

In contrast to the end of the first World War, when democracy was thought to be firmly in the saddle, it is now two great systems of political organization, democracy and bolshevism, which offer their ideas for the solution of the problems just mentioned. If both see in politics only a game of powers then there is little hope for humanity. But if they conceive of politics as of the greatest human responsibility, which consequently needs the greatest amount of unprejudiced thinking and acting together with a profound vision of the destiny of humanity, then they may finally arrive at a practical common denominator, and the rivalry between the democratic and the bolshevist ideals may turn out to be one of the most fruitful competitions of nations.

CHAPTER VII

OUTLINE OF A MODERN PHILOSOPHY

I. The Philosophies of Religious and Rational Certainty

LOOKING BACK into the development of Western thought we discover two apexes of certainty in the history of philosophical endeavor. The one is represented by the *summa theologiae* of Thomas Aquinas. In this canonical work the philosophy and theology of the Catholic Church are welded into one. The feeling of evidence which Thomas attributes to his conclusions springs less from confidence in the logical power of the human mind—however much stress he lays on rationality—than from the conviction that all true thinking about God, man, and the universe has its roots in a divine revelation in which, by the grace of the Lord, Christians are allowed to participate. Thus for Thomas, philosophy, like theology, is in the last analysis not a process of discovery, but of interpretation. The thinker would commit a sin of arrogance if, in the frailty of his human nature he attempted to explain the riddles of the universe without the help of the Divine Spirit. Philosophy, in this sense, has not yet become an independent pursuit; it serves in the role of the *ancilla theologiae*, the maid of theology. Yet from the glory of the mistress much reflects upon the servant.

The other summit of certainty on the laborious path of philosophy was reached in the period of rationalist idealism characteristic of the period from Descartes to Hegel. Rational idealism is not godless; it also believes in the embeddedness of man in the all-transcendent power of God. But whereas in traditional theology the Absolute, through an act of revelation, descends to man, according to the rationalist the human mind can grasp the truth through its own effort and ascend, as it were, up to the Absolute. Man, according to rationalist idealism, does not invent God; God is and would be, even if there were no men. But He has given us the task and the intellectual means of discovering the Divine and Eternal Law through our own endeavor. After this primary act of endowment no further special revelation is needed; all thinking is a continual act of revealing. Intellectual history, consequently, can be described as the continual striving of man for the realization of the Truth which is potentially inherent in the human mind and needs to be gradually unfolded.

This kind of rational philosophy divides itself into two main lines: one of more speculative and intuitive character, the other of more scientific empirical quality.

The great men who believed in intuitive speculation are, e.g., Confucius, Lao-tse, Plato, Spinoza, or Hegel. For them the human mind is capable of uniting itself with the One and All, to discover its laws, and to lead men to act accordingly. They all represent a form of secularized theology irrespective of whether Confucius believes in the oneness of the moral and the universal order, or whether Lao-tse and Plato opine that human ideas are rooted in a divine essence which they reflect, or whether Spinoza hopes that thinking *more geometrico* or, in other words, the application of mathematical principles to philosophy, brings man near to the divine intellect, or whether Hegel asserts that, through his discovery of the immanent dialectic of the mind, he has revealed the so-far hidden strategy and objectives of history—ultimately it is all the same. For behind all these attempts and solutions lies the faith that man can discover God in history, in nature, and most of all, in himself.

Different from this intuitional belief in the possibility of truth, but also full of enthusiastic hope, is the philosophy which since the seventeenth century emerged together with the natural sciences and had its climax in the materialist or naturalist philosophies of the nineteenth century. There were many different shades of minds among the scientific pioneers. The greatest of them, Newton, did not consider their scientific endeavor to be in contrast to religion or metaphysics, much though they fought superstition. Other scientists, however—and they were those with the greatest influence on the public mind—believed that strictly quantitative methods of research had proved to be the only instrument by which reliable statements could be ascertained about life and the universe. These scientists possessed an astounding capacity for mental self-delusion. They dismissed every problem as irrelevant which refused to be pressed into the typical categories of science, but did not hesitate to build up materialistic systems of thought claiming to explain the totality of life and the universe. The French Lamettrie and the Germans Büchner and Moleschott are characteristic representatives of this primitive type of materialistic metaphysics.

An enormous optimism works in the background of all rational philosophies, whether idealistic, scientific, or materialistic. This optimism is based on the faith, admitted or unadmitted, that man and nature have in themselves endless possibilities of development and mutual understanding. Thus we had in certain forms of philosophical idealism, as in Hegel's, or even in the medieval mysticism of Master Eckart, a theory of evolution long before the scientists attacked this problem by use of empirical research. For these intuitive thinkers evolution meant inherence of a divine element in all life which drives it to move from lower levels of being to higher ones. The lower levels contain the potentialities of the higher and the higher absorb the essential elements of the lower. Inorganic life, on the ladder of development, represents but the rung which leads up toward organic life. On the highest level of life stands man; at the same time, he reaches over into the hyper-organic. For he is able to divine God. The relation between God and nature—just as the relation between God and mind—is reciprocal; nature tries to ascend to God, but it could not do so, if God did not reach down into all existence.

The transfer of earlier intuitive forms of evolution over into the realm of observation is marked by the work of Darwin. Darwinism was the seal which science put on the gospel of progressivism, not only of the liberal, but also of the socialist type. Though coming from very different angles of experience, both liberalism and socialism of the nineteenth century were inspired by the faith that history was immanently driven toward progress. The difference being that economic liberalism saw the door toward a perfect and free society already open, whereas the attitude of socialism—also in this respect comparable to that of the early Christian church—represented a mixture of immediate pessimism with distant utopianism.

We may now look at all such dreams with the questionable maturity of an old and disillusioned man. But certain it is that their vanishing made the road free for the cynicism of dehumanized totalitarianism.

What is the reason for the present skeptical attitude with respect to all philosophies of rationalist certainty, whether they are of more idealistic, or more scientific character? One of the reasons lies in the relativism of modern research which, in the best case, ends in an attitude of tolerance without any guiding criteria as to what to tolerate or not and, in less fortunate cases, in complete indifference to any idea which rises above the level of the tangible.

But the disintegration of rationalist optimism was caused primarily by a series of historical factors: world wars, the destruction of international life and commerce, and an endless series of economic crises with consequent unemployment of large masses. Apparently destiny refused to accept as its own guiding principle the theories of nineteenth-century liberalism, progressivism, and socialist international solidarity. As a result of this disappointing experience many in whom the dream of a better world has not died out no longer adhere to the great rational systems of thought, but return for the relief of their anxious souls to mystical religions and cults. Hence a revival of Catholic Thomism, even among Protestant intellectuals in America; hence a new appreciation of churches with impressive rituals, which is not always due to a genuine inner awakening but to a desperate desire for emotional comfort and security. Hence the fact that a considerable part of money goes to palm readers, astrologers, and fortune tellers.

Certainly, genuine religion will always be one of the strongest motivating forces in civilization. It pours vigor, courage, and enthusiasm into civilization; it grows and widens with man's tasks and intuition and gives him lasting purposes. But an artificial and backward-looking form of religious revivalism is doomed to be abortive. For it is the mark of men who no longer live in the depth of life but have lost it. The anchors they throw out will not hold.

II. What Do We Know?

Therefore, before attempting to arrive at some conclusions of our own, let us first have some kind of stocktaking and find out what we really know about the fundamental problems of life and of ourselves.

In addition to the more intuitive philosophical knowledge of earlier centuries, experimental research at the end of the nineteenth century had brought together so much material that the scholars of this period could deceive themselves about the real dimensions of their knowledge. We do not need describe here what science has contributed to man's mastery of nature, to industrial efficiency, to medicine, and to many other branches of theoretical and applied scholarship. Yet, the more we have learned, the less we dare to make definite statements about the basic processes of life, especially as it expresses itself in higher forms of individuality. However much modern biology teaches us about conception and birth, for instance, it does not explain the forces which bring about life with its specific qualities of individuality and self-consciousness.

The layman who wants to have some certainty about the relationship between hereditary, innate, and acquired qualities of animals and men is told by prudent scholars that they are still far from conclusive answers. We know that purposeful behavior is the characteristic feature of organisms, especially of those endowed with brain. But we do not know how such an organism develops a purpose. If we say that it does so as a result of conditioning, we certainly describe an interesting phase in that process of formation of habit and purpose but, as we already discussed in the psychological chapter, there still remains the question as to the potentiality which enables the organism to respond to conditioning influences.

We know that living organisms from the plant upward have a certain life rhythm, but we cannot say where it comes from. We know that a normal human being possesses the power of perception and conceptualization. But though we know much about our nervous system we still are at a loss to answer the question of how an idea really emerges in the human mind, can be expressed in word-concepts, and brought into a synthetic relation to other ideas. What is going on in the process of a mental abstraction? How can we subordinate all our single impressions about birch trees, apple trees, and oak trees under the abstraction "Tree," and how can the human mind finally rise to such high abstractions as "Idea," "Ideal," "Ultimate Cause," or "God"? In other words, we know that there is something like "mind" working with the help of the organism in which it lives—though sometimes acting against its physical desires. But if somebody asks us about the old philosophical problems of the relationship betwen mind and body we can give no definite answer.

Or if the physiologist states that a surplus of income over expenditure is the indispensable condition of organic growth, he simply describes a relationship which appears to us as one between cause and effect though it may not be of that kind at all. But he does not tell us why, before grave illness and death come, the organism has the urge to wind itself up when it has run down. Is life something like will or, at least does it spring from a supreme creative and willing power?

Some people have decided to be disinterested in these problems and to rely on "observable facts." Nobody can be forbidden to decide that way. But strangely enough, no intelligent and vital person behaves in this disinterested way; instead he possesses an intense curiosity for total explanations such as strict observation alone can never give. Thus there will always be room for a large sphere of speculation behind the area of life accessible to experimental analysis and description. In this respect modern man is not different from medieval man. But he feels duty-bound to distinguish between certainty and probability. After Kant, he knows of the antinomies inherent in his intellect and of the boundaries between scientific thinking and faith. But with the very progress of knowledge modern man has experienced that science alone does not suffice to satisfy his spiritual hunger. Even when he wishes to remain within the sphere of observation and experiment he is constantly forced to make syntheses and conclusions which lead him beyond this sphere.

Thus there remains, at least for the twentieth century, nothing but a philosophical attitude which, on the one hand, is filled with an unimpeachable desire for empirical proof and critical method. On the other hand, in consequence of the very radicalness of his search for truth modern man experiences the limits of mere empiricism in the face of the great problems of the universe.[1] Either he tries to escape the challenge of these problems and thus limits his horizon, or he has to transcend the sphere of exact scientific knowledge, and

[1] I have dealt with the problem of "self-transcendent empiricism" or "transempiricism" at some length in chapter III B, of my *Fundamentals of Democratic Education* (New York: American Book Company, 1940).

form concepts which are intuitional in character. But wherever his intuition wanders, his scientific conscience will always look as a mentor over his shoulders.

III. The Great Theme of Philosophy

However, the philosophical dilemma of our time lies not only in the relationship between empirical observation and intuition, it comes from a certain stagnation in philosophy itself. When reading the typical histories of philosophy one has the impression of a man who constantly tells the story of his past and, in addition, uses a vocabulary which conceals more than it reveals, and confuses more than it clears up. For all the philosophical categories imposed upon the student such as naturalism, materialism, humanism, idealism, etc., are signposts erected on quicksands, because concepts such as nature, matter, man, and idea have no longer any clear meaning.

No doubt, in every discipline of thought there is need for a rather esoteric language; and those philosophers who are struggling with difficult problems of logic and cosmology have to use a technical language similar to that of the scientist who cannot accept the ignorance of the layman as a measure for his modes of expression. But there has always been another claim upon philosophy, namely to help thinking men in their desire for wholeness, truth, and permanence in thought and action. Different though the methods may be, in this respect philosophy has always been the twin sister of theology and always will be, however much modern "naturalists" will protest against this comparison. Either philosophy satisfies the urge of men toward a meaningful and coherent picture of life and the universe, as it did in the times when any serious student would have been ashamed to confess his philosophical ignorance, or the philosophical departments of our universities will have to be content with a small pigeonhole kindly granted them by the constantly expanding faculties of the natural and social sciences.

There are indications that these faculties discover more and more the need for a philosophical examination of their problems, but that they will satisfy this desire within their own boundaries. From the point of view of progress of knowledge this might not even be a disadvantage. But it will lead toward the result that the scientist learns only philosophy of science, the philologist philosophy of language, the art student philosophy of esthetics, and the educator philosophy of education. Thus the great ideal of a *philosophia universalis* will be buried without anybody's deeming it necessary to attend the funeral. If there is still some hope for revival, it will come only if philosophy—in the mixture of modesty and courageous effort characteristic of all great spiritual movements—reclaims a more central role in modern thought. But this claim will be acknowledged only if the new philosophy convinces modern man that it can help him solve the oldest and most comprehensive theme of human thought, namely, the quest for the meaning of existence.

IV. Existence and Experience

To this end the philosopher would show that in all physical existence, in all energy, there work two great principles: one is growth, and the other shape or form. Growth and shape occur wherever something lives or wherever energy realizes and expresses itself. Every new finding of a scientist is a contribution to the explanation of energy as it exists in growth and shape. The scientist, however, can only observe their appearances; the ultimate character of energy and existence, of growth, and shape, is a subject which requires completely new forms of co-operation between cosmology and metaphysics. But so much can already be said, that all individual being is part of a greater totality of existence. It is impossible to reject the hypothesis of a fundamental interconnection and unity of a universe which allows all things created to participate in its abounding strength until they transform themselves through death and decay into new forms of being.

But existence, like a stone, would not be interested in itself unless, at a certain stage of development, it began to know of itself. Thus we are faced with existence not only as a physical phenomenon but as experience. Also the analysis of this form of being moves toward constantly receding horizons. For every experience is like a mirror in which other mirrors reflect. It is not an enclosure with walls around it, but a disclosure that leads into the infinite.

In every great immediate experience, birth, love, death, great passion, and great danger, something like the totality of the world is present. No word can ever express it. Only minor experiences leave the ego within itself. Thus it may well be that later generations will give up our present notion of the ego or of individual existence as a primitive concept, just as mankind, in the course of its intellectual development, has been forced to give up the belief in the Ptolemaic geocentric system or in a three-dimensional reality. Today our scientists are struggling with the notion of an expanding universe, not knowing whether this idea will lead us to the conception of a closed, and finite, or an open, and infinite world. The center of the open, or infinite world, might be considered to be anywhere. Thus our concept of the universe, which first was geocentric and then heliocentric, has now become cosmic in a sense which would have been completely incomprehensible to our ancestors.

The new conception of the ego, which sooner or later is bound to emerge, would change our whole individualistic philosophy of human life into one of completely new dimensions which cannot yet be foreseen in detail. To be sure the instinctive feeling of self which every human being possesses would change as little as the Copernican discovery has modified our natural sense of stability, but psychology and philosophy would expand from man-centered toward much more universalist or cosmic conceptions. New light would be shed on the whole problem of personal attraction between two people, on mortality and immortality, and the way would be prepared for profoundly new forms of religion.

But would they really be new? Or would not the scientifically expanded aspects of the world eventually help the Western mind to understand what Lao-tse, Buddha, and Christ really meant when they spoke of the unity of man with a divine and all-permeating Spirit. If in our modern, but, alas, so terribly primitive sensualism we identify our total self with nothing but our body as we can touch, feel, clothe, and bathe it, we certainly are not "enlightened thinkers," but cut ourselves off from the depths of existence on which all the great religious prophets wished us to draw.

But whatever may happen in the sphere of abstract speculation, the knowledge of the forces which work upon and within us, will not remain the same as it is now. If before the decade of the great discoveries about radiation between 1890 and 1900 somebody had predicted X-rays and the modern development of radio and television he would have been regarded as reveling in phantasies. This whole chain of discoveries is by no means finished. Scientists will discover more and more forces in our environment and within ourselves in the light of which our present concepts about personality and experience in both their physical and experiential aspect will undergo surprising changes.

When we spoke of existence which experiences itself we always spoke, at least to a degree, of mind. The term "mind," of course, is nothing but a word-symbol for a force which we feel is working in ourselves, but which we are still unable to explain. If we used a Chinese character instead, it would be just as good. We know that mind needs tools such as our senses, brain, the nervous system, perhaps the whole body and, perhaps all that cosmic array of contacts and radiation of which we just spoke. But nobody can say whether mind itself is one of these various elements of life, or a combination of them, or whether it is something of different nature.

But in any case, this symbol expresses the capacity of the human being not only to apprehend but to understand his environment and eventually to arrive at certain principles of order within the universe, principles for the totality of which the Greeks had the name *Logos*. Whether these principles, or the *Logos*, result from man's own effort, or whether they represent a universal and superior form of being which, as it were, deigns to communicate with man, this question has always been an urgent one in the tradition of theology and philosophy. Socrates and Plato discussed it with the Sophists. Scholastic philosophy split over the conflict whether universals were God-created or man's own product, and the modern antagonism between idealism and materialism stems from the same issue.

But it seems to me that this fundamental discussion has always referred too one-sidedly to primarily intellectual problems. For the mysterious contact between the human mind and a more total world of order is not only of logical or intellectual quality. It can appear also when man experiences art and when he is engaged in intentional action, or, in other words, in esthetic and ethical situations.

Whether of course, our intellectual contact with reality is of such a kind that it grasps reality in its ultimate essence, or the *Ding an sich,* as Kant would say, nobody knows. In all likelihood it does not. Yet, the mathematical devices which we use for astronomical observations allow a surprising measure of accurate foretelling of future events in the celestial spheres; even our daily life constantly counts on an effective combination of observation, derivation, and symbolization. Thus we have ground for hope that human reason and reality are in some kind of orderly contact, though we may see the world distorted as in a badly ground mirror. In addition, much of our thought is blurred by our subjectivism with all its one-sided interests and passions. Perhaps all our thinking has an emotional and volitional basis; certainly passionateness, will, and intellect have always closely co-operated in the birth of a great product of mind and opened the eyes of the soul to ever widening aspects. Spinoza meant something like that when he coined the wonderful word of the *amor intellectualis dei*, as the highest achievement of which man is capable.

About the Truth which is in great art we have already spoken in a special chapter. It needs the whole narrowness of the verbal and intellectual Western culture to forget that Leonardo's "Mona Lisa" and Rembrandt's portraits tell us more about womanhood and manly character, and Bach's Cantatas more about the Divine than any scientific or philosophical analysis can ever do. And if we, the mere receivers or interpreters of the artists' work, already feel such approximation to the Infinite, how much more must the creative artist himself feel its afflatus?

But if the spiritual relation of man to the universe can reflect in his intellectual and artistic activities, it ought to reflect also in his intentional action and his total behavior. Thus we have ethics as the third form of contact between man and the inner order of the universe. The *summum verum*, as expressed in thought, meets in the kingdom of the Spirit not only the *summum pulchrum*, as expressed in art, but also the *summum bonum* as expressed in great deeds. For ethical action, in the deepest sense of the word, springs from man's capacity to harmonize his life with the constructive order inherent in existence. If our moral aspirations were nothing more than a coagulation of egotistic interests, then there would be no real community nor a committing idea and men would no longer have any practical interests in common. Therefore any society which believes in nothing but the rule of "well-understood interest," has alienated itself from the common spiritual background of humanity and, as history shows, is doomed to decay. Its members necessarily disperse the moment the profit motive is no longer satisfied, and then the danger of relapse into barbarism is imminent.

No doubt, the theory of well-understood interest describes correctly certain phenomena on the primarily instinctive level of human relations; but it does not explain why, at least from time to time, men felt loyalty to the idea of civilization and humanity even to the degree of self-sacrifice.

Also in modern times the gospel of self-expanding egotism marks rather the end of true liberalism and not, as some economic theorists assume, its beginning.

The previous statement about the relation of morality to a universal order does not contradict the historically proven fact that the origin of moral conduct, like the origin of all values, is in experience. For the merely historical and sociological explanation of our ethical concepts we do not need metaphysics nor a superhuman revelation. No doubt that in the course of time men discovered that it was to their own interest to conform to certain standards of common living. This is the true meaning in the assumption of a "social contract." In the long run all immoral behavior proves to be dangerous to those who indulge in it as well as to those who suffer from it. Nietzsche was right when he said that certain conventions are inventions of the weak to defend themselves against the strong. But he would have been utterly wrong if he had thought that the strong themselves could survive without morality; in fact, he never thought so.

But the fact that mankind profits from moral behavior does not warrant the conclusion that utility is the only principle which determines the universe of men and its progress, just as little as the comfort we derive from art proves that art is hedonic in nature. Rather it says that it is to the advantage of men if they act so that their action is compatible with the constructive laws in life. In other words the acting of men in accordance with the universal principles of productivity, not the profit motive, is the explanation of progress.

So, in our way, we have now arrived at the old sacred trinity of intellectual, esthetic, and ethical truth or value within one parent source, namely the mysterious contact of the human mind with the forces of growth inherent in the universe.

It is amazing how, after gaining this insight, one finds it stated again and again in all great religions and philosophies, though in different words.

Confucius says:

> When our true central self and harmony are realized, the universe then becomes a cosmos and all things attain their full growth and development.[2]

The Indian ideas of *Tat tvam asi,* the Karma, and the Nirvana express the identity of the human soul with the Living Spirit. Christ says:

> "I and the Father are one."

The conviction of a universal unity, as we already indicated, appears now even as a postulate of science. For the development of the physical sciences during the past decades compels us to expect an expansion of their merely quantitative and descriptive methodology over into a qualitative and philosophical point of view. To phrase it courageously, however much it may shock both scientists and theologians: a new form of theology will eventually emerge out of the philosophy of the natural sciences. Though this process will be revolutionary to the degree that it may mark the beginning of a new period of thought like all productive revolutions, it will nevertheless result from a long and profound evolution. The natural sciences will give up the essentials of the Newtonian method and their empirical conscience as little as theology will abandon its vision of the eternal and its mission of guidance of humanity. But through developing the postulates inherent in their thinking more and more courageously, they will not only widen their horizons, but at the same time understand and complement each other more profoundly.

Thus, though forging ahead on separate paths, they will no longer feel the customary historical discord about their

[2] *The Wisdom of Confucius,* Edited and Translated by Lin Yutang (New York: Modern Library, 1939), p. 104.

final goal. They both will recognize the abiding *Logos* within and behind the colorful, sometimes joyful and, alas, often so cruel world of appearances. This unity in variety will be the salvation of the human spirit from the terrific chaos of the present. For there are only two ways for us: either we work at this obstinate hope, or Western civilization will end in despair.

V. Our Faith

However modest we have become about the scientific validity of metaphysics, man will continue to ask about his relation to the ultimate forces in the universe. This quest has been one of his deepest concerns since he rose above the level of primitivism; he cannot suddenly stop being interested in it.

Is the force in which all life is embedded ultimately of some kind of personal character? Is it divine in the sense of "God," or in the sense of an abiding law which, as it were, has to obey itself after its self-establishment? But who established it? This question is identical with the most radical of all questions the human mind can ask: Why does existence exist, or, why is something and not nothing? This question is almost identical with another one: How can law and freedom be compatible in our universe?

The answer which can be given on scientific and philosophical grounds, has already been indicated. It is this: So far, the unity of human experience and scientific research postulates on an essentially unified, pervading, and life-spending force behind all the single appearances of existence. Some of us may envisage this force with the disciplined spirit of the scientific observer, declare any further explanation to be a futile attempt, and remain in a noble form of cool agnosticism. Others who represent the more emotional type will combine their conviction of the embeddedness of all life in an embracing and nourishing power with a deep sense of reverence and intellectual curiosity. This sense can rise to the heights of philosophical contemplation or of religious certainty which makes men believe that through contemplation, worship, and prayer they can open their souls to the inflowing grace of the Divine.

Such a belief in an ultimate identity between God and man will be a source of unspeakable enrichment and at the same time of deepest humility. In absorbing the Divine, the mystic will be absorbed by it and thus be able to expand his individual soul into the majesty of the universe.

At the base of some old sundials one can find engraved an inscription which indicates in a few words the profoundest miracle of life. It says:

"On this moment hangs eternity."

Whatever little or great things we do, we do them within a world in which nothing is lost. This is true even of our secret ideas, because a man is what he thinks, acts as he thinks, and radiates what he thinks. Therefore all the great religious leaders have laid so much stress on the systematic cultivation of our inner life; they knew that though invisible, it is the most important part of reality.

A person who acts out of such an attitude of identity between him and the universe respects himself, and yet, is humble at the same time. He acts out of inner necessity and does not expect immediate practical reward for his doing. When he uses prayer, worship, and spiritual self-education, he does not think of exercising influence on the Divine for his own immediate benefit. His prime desire is the feeling of unity from which all the other spiritual blessings follow.

For many, perhaps, such an attitude is too self-renouncing, too Stoic in character. Yet, this Stoicism does not spring from despair; rather it comes from understanding and accepting individual life as a part and phase of a continual creation. This creation contains profound joys and innumerable possibilities of development but, for the limited mind of man, it also contains the most terrific and insoluble contradictions. Why should the Eternal Order allow innocent children to be buried under the hail of bursting and burning explosives?

Why should from generation to generation the flower of mankind be killed in fighting just when it begins to ripen into sweet fruit? Why should the beauty of cities and countries, the work of centuries of human history, be destroyed overnight? Why should animals live by slaughtering other animals, and why are some of them so constructed that they enjoy playing with their prey before they kill it? Why can the same human instincts which could be turned into love and responsibility be perverted into hatred and the lust of destruction?

Again and again have these problems led the most conscientious men into the despair of nihilism and into disdain of all religious faith. Others push these disturbing problems into a hidden corner of their soul from which, however, they may suddenly emerge when unexpected catastrophes occur.

A third group of men have found comfort in reverential philosophic or religious contemplation of the divine ideas. A fourth type of man has partly forgotten himself and partly lifted himself up, by means of intense action. But they all are inferior to men such as Buddha or Christ through whom, as it were, divine grace speaks directly. Plato's and Spinoza's wisdom is the result of intensive thinking about God. Buddha's and Christ's teaching reflects their intimate being *in* God.

This is the essential and unbridgeable difference between the intellectual genius and the very few divine founders of world religions. For even in the most enthusiastic contact with the Eternal only a very, very few men can completely forget themselves. There is always some demand in their devotion, some selfishness in their absorption. As long as they remain within themselves, the universe cannot fully enter into them. But most of us have at least approximated a state of identity between ourselves and a greater universe. We can envisage what it means when a man has learned to live "inside" and no longer "outside." He lives in confidence and not in fear; he not only knows that love is greater than hatred, but lives accordingly; he suffers with those who are poor, sick and persecuted; yet he knows that seeds are growing even under scorched earth; and as the last and final result of his ripening, he discovers the meaning of the Christian symbol of the cross.

For the cross expresses this profoundest secret of life, that salvation can be found even in suffering. Perhaps the deepest salvation can be found only there, provided one also knows the salvation which is in profound joy and love. To be sure, men who have gone through this development will not seek suffering as an end in itself. Those who do so are sick—and there are more of them than we surmise. But those who have never suffered, are to be pitied too.

For acquiring this last revelation of the universe to man, thinking and teaching may be helpful. But ultimately it is the grace of faith which allows us to reach beyond our immediate reality into the deepest reality from which all other things come.

However, even in his most intimate hours of religious elevation man must not forget that these hours will perish like unfecundated flowers unless they create in his soul an increased sense for the greatness of practical social obligation. For as a plant cannot grow in pure water alone, so ideas cannot become productive unless they stem from, and end in, a profound relation and committment to those basic social conditions without which men cannot live a civilized life together.

Any philosophy or religion, therefore, which does not constantly attempt to build bridges between the realm of the Spirit and the realm of actuality fosters the kind of dualism which has allowed a minority of men to delight in the loftiness and beauty of thought and art and has left others in a life of drudgery and serfdom. This dualism has not only split whole groups of mankind into separate classes, it has also divided the soul of many an individual into parts which do not communicate with each other, one longing for salvation and often for abortive forms of sublimation, the other indulging in earthly strife and greed.

To a degree such dualism is the eternal destiny of man; much though he suffers from it. It also has provided him with the great gamut of experiences and incentives toward increasing development. But this dilemma in which man is doomed to live must turn from a state of productive into a state of unproductive tension or, which is still more, into a state of complacency if he becomes reconciled with the division of life into a sphere of "noble culture" and a sphere of "cruel reality."

Thus, at the end of this book, the circle of our considerations turns back to its beginning where it was stated that the growth of civilization is contingent upon the interaction of both the physical and the spiritual requisites of a healthy life. If the scholars, thinkers, and representatives of the churches wish to maintain their role in civilization they will have to widen the span of their interests and responsibilities far beyond the sphere to which they generally are ascribed. Not only will they have to include into their philosophizing the analysis of the totality of human life with its material, economic, political, moral, and spiritual elements, they will also have to show the ways and methods of transferring theoretical insight into practical deeds.

For only through the ever-increasing unity of thought, action, and reality can the kingdom of peace and the kingdom of truth be established on earth.

CONCLUSION

UP TO THE BEGINNING of the eighteenth century our European ancestors expressed their profoundest hopes mainly in terms which transcended the orbit of secular life. They could not think of salvation except one beyond this earthly existence with its endless struggle against sickness, hunger, and war. Johann Sebastian Bach's *Passion According to St. Matthew* is the last, and at the same time perhaps the greatest document of this permeating attitude of otherworldliness.

Again today many who have lived through the Armageddon of a world war may despair of the human capacity to create a civilized life for themselves and their children. And even those who do not know personally the horrors of destruction may sometimes recognize in the final chorale of Bach's *Passion*, that about the sleeping Christ, a voice from within crying for the dissolution of all our sins and jealousies in the soothing peace of eternity.

But there is also another voice within us, one which reminds us of the tasks and duties of modern man here on earth and within his particular society. This voice reminds us of our power over nature and over the resources of the soil, of our successes in fighting hunger and epidemics, and of the accumulation of knowledge achieved by modern man. If properly applied, all this could help him change the valleys of misery, the enforced abode of so many humans, into fields filled with the sunshine of happiness.

But why has there been so little progress?

Have we not yet enough science, and industry, not yet enough insight into the external conditions of human survival? Certainly, we could have more, and we must hope that future generations will consider our methods of life as backward as we do the life of our ancestors. Yet, we feel that if today we had all the technical skill and knowledge which future generations may amass we would not be happy. In all likelihood, just the opposite. For we are defective in one quality—*social will*.

But why has our social will—this most essential vehicle of true progress—developed so little? In trying to answer this question we find ourselves caught in a vicious circle. In order to grow, social will, as all persistent and constructive trends, needs a conducive environment. But the environment of man, so far, has been determined mainly by the fight against the hardships of nature, or it has been competitive, a struggle for survival covering the whole gamut from barbaric to highly refined, but not less dangerous, forms of rivalry.

Certainly, this cruel character of our environment has been one important reason for the discrepancy between the intellectual-technical and the social progress of man.

However, no great stride was ever made in human evolution which did not have to break through some kind of vicious circle. Pessimists can always point at the apparent helplessness of the situation. But the daring man will answer: begin somewhere, each on the spot where destiny has placed you. Do not wait for the ringing of a bell which suddenly announces a great mission, but start yourself, in your daily work, and in your relations to your neighbor. The blessing of this attitude will radiate much farther than you think.

Environment is not only fate. Certainly the struggle with the things around has kept man from being fully human, but so has man himself. This not so much because he is of evil intention—a normal and healthy person rather prefers kindness to malice—but because he is so terribly ignorant about the conditions of his own and his fellow men's happiness.

Or, instead of ignorance, should we not better blame unconscious narrowness and one-sidedness as the causes of our social deficiency? For they are the dangers which threaten to lead into prejudice not only the untrained mind, but also the intelligent and educated.

We are so narrow and one-sided because after learning how to master nature we have neglected to learn how to master ourselves and to see where the roots of our total existence are. Thus the period of technology has become a period of superficiality, ending in the greatest destruction of goods which mankind ever wrought upon itself.

Hence, together with the progress of engineering and industrialization, which may bring better housing and food for more and more people, we have to acquire a more profound and comprehensive image of man. For this we need the wisdom and depth which is in the awareness of the transcendent forces of life just as much as we need a rational and empirical attitude. In many respects man is, and will always be, exposed to the dangers and abysses of his own nature, because it is part of a greater nature which is not only grand and beautiful, but also cruel. Thus, in order to understand himself in his totality and to dissolve his narrower in his profounder desires, man needs the depths of insight and experience which religion can give him just as much as he needs progress in science; he needs Bach's *Passion According to St. Matthew* as much as the blessings of modern hygiene.

In other words, for the development of a universal social will, he will have to burst the hoops of narrowness and abandon isolating attitudes and concepts which shut the windows of the soul to wider vistas. Either we decide for the road toward gigantic synthesis, or we will go the road toward destruction. If we only learn to make bigger and bigger machines without growing proportionately in full human size we will become increasingly enmeshed in our egotisms and turn our weapons against each other for the final victory of death over life, of barbarism over civilization. Let us repeat the *Leitmotiv* of this whole book:

Man has become too powerful, and the earth has become too small to allow him the unwise use of his power. He has to choose either the great decay, or the great embrace. There is nothing in between.

INDEX